BROTHERS, SISTERS, AND SPECIAL NEEDS

BROTHERS, SISTERS, AND SPECIAL NEEDS

Information and Activities for Helping Young Siblings of Children with Chronic Illnesses and Developmental Disabilities

by

Debra J. Lobato, Ph.D.

Director of Psychology
Child Development Center
Rhode Island Hospital
and
Assistant Professor
Department of Pediatrics
Brown University Program in Medicine
Providence

Photographs by Ricardo D. Barrera
Line drawings by Philip J. Leonard, III

·P A U L ·H ·
BROOKES
PUBLISHING CO.

Baltimore • London • Toronto • Syd

Paul H. Brookes Publishing Co.
P.O. Box 10624
Baltimore, Maryland 21285-0624

Typeset by Brushwood Graphics, Inc., Baltimore, Maryland.
Manufactured in the United States of America by
The Maple Press Company, York, Pennsylvania.

Second printing, September 1993.

'ongress Cataloging-in-Publication Data

 J., 1954–
    s, and special needs : information and activities
   g siblings of children with chronic illnesses and
    'sabilities / Debra J. Lobato.

      phical references (p.
       '-3 :
          dren—Family relationships.   2. Developmentally
          nily relationships.   3. Brothers and sisters.

                                              90-1518
                                              CIP

ney

CONTENTS

Paul H. Brookes Publishing Co.
P.O. Box 10624
Baltimore, Maryland 21285-0624

Typeset by Brushwood Graphics, Inc., Baltimore, Maryland.
Manufactured in the United States of America by
The Maple Press Company, York, Pennsylvania.

Second printing, September 1993.

Library of Congress Cataloging-in-Publication Data

Lobato, Debra J., 1954–
Brothers, sisters, and special needs : information and activities
for helping young siblings of children with chronic illnesses and
developmental disabilities / Debra J. Lobato.
   p.   cm.
   Includes bibliographical references (p.
   ISBN 1-55766-043-3 :
    1. Chronically ill children—Family relationships.   2. Developmentally
disabled children—Family relationships.   3. Brothers and sisters.
4. Counseling. I. Title.
RJ380.L63   1990
362.3′3—dc20   90-1518
                                        CIP

BROTHERS, SISTERS, AND SPECIAL NEEDS

Information and Activities for Helping
Young Siblings of Children with Chronic
Illnesses and Developmental Disabilities

by

Debra J. Lobato, Ph.D.

Director of Psychology
Child Development Center
Rhode Island Hospital

and

Assistant Professor
Department of Pediatrics
Brown University Program in Medicine
Providence

Photographs by Ricardo D. Barrera
Line drawings by Philip J. Leonard, III

·P A U L·H·
BROOKES
PUBLISHING C°

Baltimore • London • Toronto • Sydney

FOREWORD

IN MY WORK AT SPECIAL OLYMPICS, I HAVE SEEN HOW SENSITIVELY AND ENTHUSIASTI-cally the brothers and sisters of our athletes respond when they are given a clear and satisfying role. They play with their brothers and sisters. They coach them, encourage them, give them attention and great caring.

Very often, however, *their* needs are overlooked. While everyone else is paying close and constant attention to their brother or sister, while special programs and events seem to focus on that child, these generous and loving siblings often ask, "What about me?".

Debra Lobato's very comprehensive book answers this question and many more. It gives parents more than "expert" answers to their questions and problems. It is filled with insight, knowledge, and practical solutions. Dr. Lobato understands that the needs of the family can be just as compelling as the individual needs of the special child.

With this book, families have a treasury of good ideas and activities that work. If families will follow her guidance, no brother or sister need ask again, "What about me?".

Eunice Kennedy Shriver
Founder and Honorary Chairman
Special Olympics International

PREFACE

EACH DAY, WITHIN MANY PEDIATRIC AND SPECIAL EDUCATION FACILITIES, CHILDREN with their parents and siblings seek information and treatment of various medical and/or developmental problems. A wide range of relationships and behavior among the siblings exists. There are the young brothers and sisters who appear unimpressed by their hospital or school surroundings, or by their siblings' illness or disability. They express much the same mix of love and hostility in the waiting rooms as would many other brothers and sisters in the living rooms of their homes. There are also the young siblings who hover close to their brothers or sisters, consoling them and their parents through difficult procedures or praising them after successful therapy sessions. And then there are the siblings who do not accompany their brothers and sisters to scheduled visits as they are cared for by someone else, or are busy with other activities. While these children and their families are all unique, they express some common questions and needs regarding their brothers' and sisters' problems. Their parents want to know how to explain and respond to the child's special needs in a way that is both informative and sensitive to the sibling's own needs. While parents want to help all of their children understand and adapt to the situation as fully as possible, knowing just how to go about this is not always clear.

The purpose of *Brothers, Sisters, and Special Needs: Information and Activities for Helping Young Siblings of Children with Chronic Illnesses and Developmental Disabilities* is to provide information to parents and professionals so that they may best understand and address the unique and common needs of young brothers and sisters of children with significant developmental disabilities and chronic illnesses. The book has two major sections. The first four chapters review literature relevant to understanding sibling relationships in general and how they may be affected by a child's chronic illness or disability. Practical information on educational and support services for siblings appears in the second half of the book.

The first chapter of the book provides background information on how typical young brothers or sisters usually influence one another's development. Chapter 2 explores the special experiences of young children whose brothers or sisters have a chronic illness or developmental disability. Common conceptions and misconceptions among young siblings regarding medical and developmental problems and their family's adaptation to them are examined. Chapters 3 and 4 summarize the professional literature regarding the psychological adjustment of brothers and sisters of children who have a wide variety of medical and developmental problems. Particular attention is paid to understanding why some children appear to adapt well and feel benefited by the experience while other children feel they and their families generally have been harmed.

The second half of the book contains very practical, concrete strategies that parents and professionals can use to identify and address young siblings' needs at home and via a sibling workshop series. Chapter 5 describes the range of services that have been developed to date for brothers and sisters, including interventions such as discussion groups, family support groups, and sibling tutoring. Chapter 6 identifies step-by-step the factors that should by considered when deciding to run a sibling workshop program. Following these general guidelines for organizing and planning a workshop program is a specific curriculum for addressing the needs of young siblings in Chapter 7. This workshop series is a group activity designed to increase young children's understanding of developmental disabilities and chronic illnesses in general, to increase their understanding of their own brothers' or sisters' problems, to increase their recognition of their own and other family members' strengths, to encourage their expression of positive and negative emotional reactions to the stressful events related to their brothers' or sisters' illnesses, and to provide them with emotional support by discussing these issues and participating in activities with other young brothers and sisters. Chapter 8 gives specific suggestions for program evaluation. Techniques for collecting consumer satisfaction data from parents and siblings as well as evaluating siblings' attitudes and behavior at home are provided. Chapter 9 offers parents and professionals general and specific guidelines for explaining medical and developmental problems to young children. While adults often agree to provide simple, honest explanations to children, they do not always know how much or what type of information is most appropriate for young preschool-age children. Chapter 9 also lists definitions of many disabilities and chronic illnesses in terms that young children can understand. To further assist parents and professionals in explaining medical and developmental problems to young children, a review of children's literature regarding disabilities and illnesses appears in the Annotated Bibliography.

The information contained within *Brothers, Sisters, and Special Needs* reflects years of clinical and research experience with young children and their families. My ability to create and organize the activities has been fueled by the interest, dedication, and enthusiasm of the many parents and children with whom I have had the pleasure of working. Some parents served as transportation coordinators for siblings participating in early workshop groups, others provided regular feedback about their children's participation, while others opened their hearts and homes so that the photographs contained herein could be captured and shared by others. Their generosity over the years will always be remembered and admired.

As services for children with developmental and medical needs become increasingly family-oriented and home-based, the needs of their young brothers and sisters will become more apparent as well. It is hoped that the information and activities contained in this volume will enable parents and professionals to recognize the special role brothers and sisters play in one another's health and development and to provide the opportunities and support necessary to strengthen this special role.

To my mother and father

CHAPTER 1

UNDERSTANDING
SIBLING RELATIONSHIPS

RELATIONSHIPS BETWEEN BROTHERS AND SISTERS ARE among the most rich and enduring bonds that children and adults experience. Brothers and sisters generally spend more time with one another than they do with their parents, not only during childhood, but throughout the course of their lives (Brody & Stoneman, 1986; Lawson & Ingleby, 1974). Most children grow up with siblings, and in many cultures they are raised by siblings (Dunn, 1985). When parents are asked why they choose to have a second child, most say that the primary reason is that they do not want their firstborn to be an only child. Right or wrong, people tend to believe that children develop best within the company of other children. What is it that is so special about sibling relationships? What is it that children learn and do with their siblings that they don't do with their parents and friends?

The purpose of this chapter is to explore the nature of typical sibling relationships in order to provide a foundation and perspective for understanding the effects of a child's chronic illness or disability on his or her nonhandicapped siblings. The author examines the significance of siblings and the functions that their relationships play in children's development. The author focuses closely on the relationships between young brothers and sisters—those in their infancy, preschool, and early elementary school years. The range of interactions and issues that they and their parents face is examined.

SIGNIFICANCE OF SIBLINGS

Many scholars believe that brothers and sisters actively shape one another's lives and prepare each other for the experiences that they will have with peers and as adults. The major areas of influence or functions of siblings are outlined in Table 1.1. These include siblings' contribution to one another's development, their influence on one another's relationships and experiences with other people, and the type of knowledge about the world that children gain more readily from their siblings than parents.

Developmental Importance

The relationships that brothers and sisters have with one another are quite different from those that they have with their parents, pri-

Table 1.1. Functions of sibling relationships

Developmental importance
Emotional experiences and expression
  Love
  Affection
  Intimacy
  Companionship
  Competition
  Rivalry
  Jealousy/envy
  Resentment
Social experiences and skills
  Caregiving
  Negotiation
  Play
  Sharing
  Fighting/impulse control
  Compromise
Personality
  Self-identity
  Sibling constellation effects
Language and motor milestones

Influences on relationships with others
Distribution of family resources
Setting expectations
Pioneering
Maintaining secrecy and alliances
Translating

Teaching: Disseminating information
Peer
Dating
Modern culture (e.g., fashion, music, toys)

marily in the relative amount of power held by the members of the pair. In the typical adult-child interaction, the adult is at an advantage since he or she possesses greater knowledge, experience, and control over the ultimate outcome of the exchange. The adult maintains control over a higher proportion of the potential privileges and rewards that the child desires. In contrast, in the sibling pair (especially of children close in age and ability), the children are at a more equal footing. They are more likely to desire the same things at the same time and to have equal access, if not entitlement, to them. This greater similarity between siblings in their desire and power provides fertile ground for conflict and conflict resolution. Therefore, some of the earliest lessons children learn about sharing, competition, rivalry, and compromise are learned through their negotiations with siblings. In order to establish harmony and to avoid negative interference from parents, siblings must learn to settle disagreements peacefully. However, even when siblings do not succeed at reaching peaceful solutions to their differences, they can benefit indirectly from having to learn to cope with the frustration and to control the feelings of hostility. Disagreements and physical fighting are far more common between siblings than between children outside the family (Newson & Newson, 1970, 1976). Fighting and hostility between siblings occur even among the most affectionate and loving pairs (Dunn, 1985). Some of this comes from the degree of intimacy that siblings share. By living together under similar rule, siblings come to know exactly what each other is sensitive to and how to provoke whatever reaction is wanted.

Unlike earlier views of siblings only as rivals, current research on typical siblings highlights the full range of positive and negative emotions that characterizes the relationship. Children can experience feelings of affection and intense loyalty toward another person of similar age and ability. It is this last emotion—loyalty—that often distinguishes the relationship between siblings and friends (Bank & Kahn, 1982). When most adults think back on their childhoods, they can recall moments when they gladly would have given away their brothers or sisters. However, if another person from outside the family dared to criticize or threaten the child, then the sibling was often the first one to that child's defense. This ability to love and defend, despite occasional feelings of hostility and anger, captures the unique quality of the sibling relationship.

In addition to their lessons of companionship and sharing, siblings also experience the role of parents as they take care of and provide for one another's emotional and physical needs. Older children help care for younger ones, and vise versa, and thereby provide one another with a taste of some of the responsibilities of parenthood. Though this is especially apparent among older siblings, it is also apparent as early as the toddler years. Following the birth of a new baby, there is often an increase in a toddler or preschool age sibling's interest in and play with dolls. Much of the play parallels the caregiving of the newborn, with much focus on diapering, feeding, and putting the doll to sleep (Dunn, 1985). When a young child is distressed and only an older sibling is available, the child is likely to go to the sibling for comfort and consolation. The older sibling, in turn, is likely to provide it.

Siblings are important to each others' self-identity and personality development as well. It is common to hear someone make a comment such as, "My sister is like my father and I'm like my mother" or, "My brother is very creative but I'm not." Both statements reflect how people define themselves in relation to some characteristic of a brother or sister. It is also common for others to define and characterize children in relationship to each other. Parents often are guilty of such comparisons. One mother describes her two daughters by saying that her secondborn "isn't nearly as outgoing as my first." Rather than describing the second child on her own terms, the mother uses the firstborn child as the point of reference. In some cases the comparisons are taken as flattery, but often they can become a source of resentment.

The effect of sibling constellation factors, especially birth order, on children's development has been an area of great scientific and popular interest, though its effects are actually quite limited (Sutton-Smith, 1982). Birth order alone determines little in a child's development but is influential when considered along with other features of the sibling group. Though there are huge individual and family differences, firstborn children are generally characterized as being more high achieving, dominant, conservative, and socially-anxious. In contrast, laterborn children are described as more relaxed and popular, more flexible in their thinking, yet not quite as eminent in their achievements. It is likely that some of these birth order differences have their roots in the differences in the behavior of most parents with their first- and laterborn children and with children of different genders. Firstborn children generally receive more attention from their parents than laterborns, not only before the other children come along, but also when mothers are observed alone with their first- and laterborn children (Dunn & Kendrick, 1982). Mothers tend to expect, talk to, and interact verbally more with firstborns, yet tend to be more physically nurturant and indulgent of laterborns. Laterborns generally receive less pressure to become independent and are allowed indulgences such as later bedtimes and toilet training attempts (Newson & Newson, 1970, 1976). The way in which children argue and try to control others within the family is also influenced by birth order (Sutton-Smith & Rosenberg, 1970). Firstborns are more likely to be verbally aggressive and domineering, while laterborns are more likely to be physically aggressive and to recruit parents to their defense. They are also more likely to try to win an argument by begging and pleading. For the parents' part, they are three times more likely to defend the younger sibling in a disagreement even when they have little knowledge of the events surrounding the problem (Dunn, 1985).

One clear difference between first- and laterborn children lies in their language development. Perhaps due to their exclusive attention from parents, firstborns generally begin to speak earlier in life than other children in the family. Children raised in large groups, who presumably hear more speech from other children than from adults, also are slower in achieving language milestones (Dunn, 1985).

In addition to simple birth order effects, other important aspects of the sibling group include age spacing between the children and whether the group is of mixed gender. Studies on age-spacing reveal that there is more affection with less rivalry or hostility when children are spaced 4 years or more apart. Wider age-spacing also is associated with less parental stress and reports of better marital relationships (Wagner, Schubert, & Schubert, 1985). The data regarding children in mixed-gender versus same-gender siblings is conflicting. Some researchers have reported the greatest degree of rivalry and jealousy in same-gender pairs (Wagner et al., 1985), while others have reported the most positive relationships within this group (Abramovitch, Corter, & Pepler, 1980). Thus, the direct influence of siblings on one another's social, emotional, and personality development is strong.

Influences on Relationships with Others

One of the most powerful influences that siblings have on one another is their ability to affect each others' relationships with other people. This applies not only to their parents, but to other adults and children outside of the family as well.

When another child is born, the family's resources of time, energy, and finances are redistributed. While an only child has exclusive access to parents' offerings, groups of children obviously are going to have to share whatever exists. The change in the distribution of family resources is most remarkable for the firstborn child with the birth of a second child. The contrast in parent-child relationships and the distribution of family resources is generally much less dramatic for second- or laterborn children. When young firstborns' behavior with their mothers is compared before and after the baby's arrival, there is a dramatic decrease in the amount of time the mother talks to and plays with the child. Mothers initiate less interaction with the child than previously and the child often has to initiate an interaction for one to occur. Relatedly, there is also an increase in the amount of conflict between the child and parents with typical increases in whining, tearful, demanding behaviors, and temper tantrums on the child's part. Additionally, there is a dramatic increase in the frequency of the firstborn's "deliberate naughtiness," especially when his or her mother is directly involved with such activities as feeding or diapering the new baby (Dunn & Kendrick, 1982). Thus, a baby's birth can dramatically affect an older (especially a firstborn) child's behavior and experience with parents. Interestingly, the children who show the greatest distress following the birth of a new sibling are those who had particularly close and playful relationships with their mothers prior to the baby's birth (Dunn &

Kendrick, 1982). There are great differences in the ways in which mothers spend time at home with their firstborns (Abramovitch, Pepler, & Corter, 1982). Some mothers and children interact frequently and play a great deal, while other children spend their days wandering around the house while their mothers take care of other responsibilities. The latter children receive relatively less frequent and intense attention from their mothers to begin with, so perhaps there is less of a contrast and adjustment for them to make after a new child arrives. Parents appear to ease the transition for firstborns and to encourage affection from them toward the baby by including the first child in small ways in the care of the baby. Also, by explaining the baby's behaviors and feelings as a person and full member of the family, parents may engender more considerate, prosocial behavior in the firstborn (Dunn, 1985; Dunn, Kendrick, & MacNamee, 1981).

Expectations of children born later in a family are influenced by the behavior of the older siblings. The pressure that these expectations exert can be both positive and negative for laterborns. Some of the positive benefits relate to the pioneering efforts of earlierborn siblings with respect to privileges. It is quite common for older children to demand that younger ones thank them for "breaking their parents in." Younger children are indulged certain privileges earlier

in life due to the maverick efforts of their older siblings. They experience considerably more relaxed and flexible parents than do the earlierborn children. Children set standards of behavior that parents and teachers often use in evaluating the performance of a different child within the family. For example, one child who brings home average grades is interrogated as to why he or she doesn't get straight "A's" like the brother or sister, or a teacher prejudges one child on the basis of the reputation for problems in a sibling.

Within most families, siblings are known to form alliances with each other or their parents in order to exert influence over certain aspects of family governance. Siblings can intervene as a parent is about to reward or punish another child in the family and, thereby influence discipline and parenting. For example, one child can tattle on another, informing his or her parents about some misdeed they would not have realized otherwise. With that one act, the sibling can increase the parents' dissatisfaction with the other child and increase that child's likelihood of punishment. Similarly, the sibling can maintain another's secret or align with the child in a lie to their parents about a misdeed that decreases the likelihood of punishment. Alternatively, siblings can brag about one another's accomplishments and bring them to the attention of their parents, changing the adults' perspective of both children.

One important function that siblings play for one another is that of translator across the generations. Older siblings often act as go-betweens in disputes between their parents and younger siblings. They try to explain the behavior of one to the other. The greater experience or trials older siblings have with their parents enables them to explain family rules to younger children. Likewise, being children themselves, albeit with slightly greater status in the family, older children can help parents understand the younger children's ideas, concerns, and experiences. When an 8-year-old boy tells his parents that his 5-year-old brother should be allowed to wear "high top sneakers because that's what the other kindergarten kids wear," the 8-year-old is serving as a moderator. He is helping his parents understand the younger child's position more clearly.

Teaching

There are certain lessons that children are more likely to learn from their siblings and peers than from their parents. These relate to many aspects of modern culture, including music, fashion, and toys; peer relationships; and dealings with people of the opposite gender. Siblings advise one another about friendships, reputations, whom they should date, and what they should and should not do on their dates. Children's taste in things such as music, fashion, and other hobbies are more similar to their siblings' than their parents' (Koch, 1960). Their shared culture, interests, and experiences can form a foundation of a lifetime of companionship.

YOUNG SIBLING RELATIONSHIPS: OBSERVATIONS AND INTERVIEWS

Some of the most interesting and useful information regarding relationships between brothers and sisters has come from observational research—projects in which the interactions between the children were observed and recorded rather than simply described by their parents (Abramovitch, Corter, & Lando, 1979; Abramovitch et al., 1982; Dunn, 1985; Dunn & Kendrick, 1982). Additionally, talking to very young children about their brothers and sisters has provided amusing and revealing insights into how young children process their sibling experiences on an emotional and intellectual level.

Toddlers and Preschoolers

There are certain characteristics of sibling interaction during the preschool years that are quite unique to that period. The distinctive features of interactions between very young brothers and sisters include very high rates of imitation and co-action (i.e., doing the same thing at the same time) and the uninhibited, rapidly shifting emotional quality of the relationship (Abramovitch et al., 1982; Dunn, 1985). Obviously, it is during the early years when the issues regarding the effect of a new baby are going to be acute. Not only can such a birth be a source of distress but it can also be the subject of intense curiosity and interest as well. Older preschool-age children generally are so very intrigued by a newborn that during the initial weeks following the baby's birth, preschoolers spend a substantial amount of time hovering over and observing the baby, imitating its moves and facial grimaces (Dunn & Kendrick, 1982). As the baby matures into a toddler, he or she becomes the observer and imitator while the older child often assumes the role of model and manager (Abramovitch et al., 1982). Observations of young sibling pairs at home show that the younger members of the sibling group engage in almost 80% of the imitation that occurs. They imitate the older children's desirable skills as well as their playful, silly behaviors.

When observed together at home, young siblings interact frequently and show a wide range of prosocial and antagonistic behaviors with one another. While preschool siblings are rarely physically aggressive toward newborn brothers and sisters, the baby's presence does increase preschoolers' aggression toward their mothers. However, once the baby nears its first birthdate, direct and seemingly deliberate aggression from the preschoolers toward the baby is more common, especially among boys. In one study, older siblings initiated more than 80% of the antagonistic or negative interactions that occurred between the youngsters. As time passes, the younger brothers and sisters of the more aggressive siblings tend to show higher rates of counter-aggression as well (Abramovitch et al., 1982; Dunn & Kendrick, 1982).

In addition to the antagonistic behavior between young siblings are equally frequent occurrences of heart-warming, positive interactions. Older siblings tend to initiate more positive behavior than their younger brothers and sisters (Abramovitch et al., 1982; Dunn & Kendrick, 1982). Both older and younger children, even as young as 14 months, can provide comfort to the other in distress. Preschoolage siblings often introduce their younger brothers and sisters to extended imaginative play. Older siblings are almost always responsible for initiating and organizing games when the younger child is below 3 years of age. By 3 years old, however, younger siblings are more skillful in their play and more often initiate extended games and can develop roles within their games for themselves and their older siblings to take (Dunn, 1985). Common during the preschool years are "mismatches" in the behavior of two siblings. While one demonstrates frequently friendly behavior, the other is more openly hostile. According to Dunn (1985), this type of mismatch occurs in about 20% of the interactions between preschool-toddler siblings.

In some families, interactions between the young siblings fall into patterns of generally antagonistic behavior with some coopera-

tion, while others are typically friendly and affectionate with rare occurrences of aggression. Other pairs alternate frequently and intensely between the two. Most research shows that the emotional quality of the children's early relationships with one another is rather stable (Abramovitch et al., 1982; Dunn, 1985). Children who predominantly express affection toward their siblings are most likely to do so during their early childhood years. The amount of imitation of firstborn children by younger siblings suggests that the response of the older child toward the birth of the baby is a pretty good indicator of how the children may get along during their early childhood (Dunn, 1985; Dunn & Kendrick, 1982).

Though preschool-age siblings exhibit a substantial amount of positive, affectionate behavior toward one another, when given the opportunity to talk about their brothers and sisters, preschoolers tend to be very unfriendly in their choice of words (Bigner, 1974; Dunn, 1985; Dunn & Kendrick, 1982; Koch, 1960). It should be kept in mind that preschoolers use words differently than adults. Their words do not always have the same meaning or impact. For example, children use very emotional, uninhibited language when they talk about and interact with their brothers and sisters. It is not at all unusual for a preschooler to scream, "I hate you! I'm never playing with you again," at one moment and then to return within 5 minutes to see if the sibling wants to go out and play.

In their descriptions of their brothers and sisters, preschoolers often appear unaware of the personal strengths that their siblings possess. Preschoolers' evaluations of their siblings are generally very self-centered. In fact, even when preschoolers are cornered into describing something good about a sibling, they are likely to describe actions that resulted in a direct benefit to themselves. For example, when a group of 4- and 5-year-olds were asked to describe their brothers' and sisters' positive qualities, they produced the following "flattering" compliments:

"Well, my sister takes me bike riding."
"He sometimes lets me play with his toys."
"He make me ice cream."
"Well, Mommy doesn't have to change her diaper anymore."

In addition to the self-centered perspectives of their siblings, preschoolers also are very concrete in what they pay attention to and recall. They do not evaluate abstract personal qualities of the sibling as a person (e.g., you should not expect to hear a preschooler describe her sister as generous or intelligent). Rather, preschoolers typically pay attention to and react to their siblings' overt behavior in specific situations. An exception, however, is that youngsters tend to use more sophisticated and abstract terms to describe what they dislike about a sibling. For example, young children often describe their siblings as being "mean" or "bad."

As they mature, siblings begin to evaluate one another in more sophisticated and refined ways. Additionally, the nature of their behavior together evolves as well.

Early Childhood

Follow-up studies of children show that the sheer amount of interaction between siblings generally increases as they enter early childhood (Abramovitch et al., 1982; Dunn & Kendrick, 1982). As during their preschool years, older siblings tend to initiate more of the positive interactions than their younger siblings, though the younger children become a more equal partner as time goes on. Older siblings tend to initiate more verbal aggression while the younger siblings rely more on physical attacks and appeals to parents during sibling conflicts. The overall amount of aggression between brothers and sisters tends to decrease with age, though siblings still are significantly more aggressive with one another than they are with children outside the family (Newson & Newson, 1970, 1976). As children get older, their aggression and hostility are more likely to be expressed verbally in the forms of insults, ridicule, and belittling of one another's performance.

As siblings enter early childhood they begin to encounter unique social experiences outside the family that they likely may not share. The child entering school has greater capacity and opportunity to develop an identity with peers and other adults that is distinctly different from his or her role within the family. Rivalry and competition in relation to parent attention and affection can be replaced with competition regarding achievements and performance in other arenas. So, for example, the older child can aspire to competence in the classroom and be less threatened by the younger child's increasing competence within the family. However, they may begin to compete in another area such as sports. During early childhood, siblings more often challenge one another to be more physically active and daring, especially boys (Bryant, 1982; Longstreth, Longstreth, Ramirez, & Fernandez, 1975). Older siblings, especially girls, assume effective teaching and caregiving roles with younger siblings, which the latter can perceive as domineering and bossy. In their attempts to teach and provide care, older sisters often encourage dependency in the younger child. Older siblings' roles as caregivers and managers of younger children are encouraged more by parents as the older children enter middle childhood.

It is also during these years that siblings begin to exert some influence over one another's interests and preferences. Through their broadening contacts outside the family, siblings can begin to introduce aspects of modern culture into the family with an effect that parents cannot truly rival. During early childhood, siblings can begin to provide true companionship to one another. When they have new experiences they are better able than before to talk about them together and to understand each other's differing perspectives.

As children near their 7th or 8th birthday, they become somewhat less self-centered and negative in their descriptions of their brothers and sisters. Though they still use more emotional and negative tones when describing their brothers or sisters than when they describe other family members, they more readily express their positive personal attributes. For example, an 8-year-old girl states that her 4-year-old sister "is good at gymnastics, for her age."

These "older" youngsters express more appreciation for the companionship that a sibling brings. One 7-year-old boy states, "I would hate to be an only child. Then I'd have nobody to play with after school." In the next breath, however, that same child complains that his 4-year-old brother is a "stupid crybaby" because he gets tearful and whines when the brother leaves their house for the morning school bus.

Another development during early childhood in siblings' understanding of each other is the emergence of an appreciation for the multiple effects of all family members on each other. For example, an 8-year-old explains that her 3-year-old sister turns to her for comfort: "Whenever Mommy and Daddy argue, we go downstairs and play real quiet. Then she won't go bother them and get 'em more mad."

SUMMARY

From birth onward, brothers and sisters play important roles in all aspects of each other's development. They influence each other's social experiences both within and beyond the family. Characteristic of the interactions between young brothers and sisters are intense, uninhibited expressions of the full range of human emotion—from love, affection, and loyalty to hatred, hostility, and resentment. Though particular sibling groups tend toward one emotional tone or the other, experiences of both positive and negative feelings and behaviors are a guaranteed reality of all siblings' relationships. Just how this very volatile, yet stable, aspect of childhood is affected by the experience of one child's developmental or medical problems is, of course, the focus of the remainder of this book.

CHAPTER 2

EXPERIENCES
OF SPECIAL SIBLINGS

WHEN GROSSMAN (1972) COMPLETED THE RESULTS OF HER study of the college-age siblings of children with mental retardation, she found that nearly one-half of the young adults felt that they had benefited overall from their family experiences, while an equal percentage felt that they had been harmed. Those who had benefited and coped well with the situation were judged to possess many of the most admirable of human qualities. As young adults, these siblings of children with mental retardation were described as having a greater understanding and compassion for others, and more sensitivity toward prejudices. Additionally, they were more tolerant of people, especially those with disabilities, and were more likely than their peers to appreciate their own good health and intelligence.

In contrast, those college students who were judged as having been harmed overall by being raised with a child with mental retardation reported quite different experiences. Among this group were young people who felt shame about their brother or sister who was handicapped. They felt neglected by their parents whom they saw as preoccupied and consumed with the care of their sibling with mental retardation. These students blamed the child's mental retardation for placing stress on the parents' relationship and the family as a whole.

As can be seen, the experience of these different siblings reflect the opposite sides of the spectrum. Where one sibling reported feeling proud of the accomplishments of the child with mental retardation, another reported feeling embarrassed by his or her inabilities. Where one sibling found closeness and unity in the family, another found distance and isolation.

The range of possible positive and negative feelings and characteristics associated with being raised with a child with a handicap or chronic illness are outlined in Table 2.1. This list is based primarily on interviews or essays in which teenagers and adults reflect upon and describe the ways in which they feel their lives have been affected by their brothers' or sisters' problems (Caldwell & Guze, 1960; Cleveland & Miller, 1977; Gogan & Slavin, 1981; Graliker, Fischler, & Koch, 1962; Grossman, 1972; Hayden, 1974; Klein, 1972; Sullivan, 1979; Wilson, Blacher, & Baker, 1989). Though adults report feeling that they were generally either benefited or harmed by their family uniqueness, all report that they felt the full range of emotional effects at one point or another in their lives.

Table 2.1. Effects of the child with handicaps or chronic illness on brothers and sisters

Potential positive effects

Maturity
Responsibility
Altruism
Tolerance
Humanitarian concerns and careers
Sense of closeness in the family
Self-confidence and independence

Potential negative effects

Feelings of parental neglect
Feelings of resentment
Perceived parental demands and expectations for achievement
Embarrassment
Guilt about own health
Extra responsibility in the home
Restrictions in social activity
Sense of distance in the family

The roots of the feelings and perceptions of adolescent and adult siblings lie in their early childhoods. To be sure of this fact, however, the questions should be asked: What feelings do young siblings express about their brothers and sisters, and how are their interactions together affected by one's illness or disability? What are some of the unique stressors and challenges that young siblings encounter as a function of their brothers' or sisters' conditions?

TALKING TO YOUNG SIBLINGS

When two groups of children between the ages of 3 and 8 years were asked to describe their healthy, normal siblings and their brothers or sisters with chronic illnesses or disablities, there were no significant differences in the way they described them (Lobato, Barbour, Hall, & Miller, 1987). Read the words of the young children below as they answer the question, "Tell me about your brother or sister." See if you can figure out which ones are talking about a child with a significant health or developmental problem.

Rachel (4 years old) describes Steven (18 months old): *"He likes to walk and crawl and take lots of naps. He watches TV, sometimes he sits with me. We play together a lot but sometimes he knocks down my towers, but then I build new ones and he knocks them down while I'm building them, too."*

Jonah (5 years old) describes Larry (3 years old): *"He walks a lot, looks at books, gets new toys and he watches TV too much. Sometimes my mother makes him sad—lots of times, really."*

Molly (4 years old) describes Zachary (2 years old): *"He plays with me and he's mostly cranky. That's all I know about him."*

Sarah (5 years old) describes Tina (1 year old): *"She's cute and nice. She usually makes a face like this (demonstrates). Her eyes are bright and shiny. She has blonde hair and she's a baby."*

Douglas (6 years old) describes Russell (3 years old): *"Yucky, that's all he is. That's all I have to say about him. Whenever you turn your back he's in trouble . . . ."*

Heather (3 years old) describes Cara (7 years old): *"Her plays with her friends. Her's bigger than me. She gots blue eyes. Her loves me."*

Chances are that you could not tell that the first three children were talking about their normal, healthy brothers, while the last three children were describing siblings with multiple medical problems, hyperactivity, and mental retardation, respectively. As you can see, very young children often do not even refer to their brother's or sister's medical problems or special needs when they describe them to others. Rather, at a young age, siblings focus on the children's actions, appearance, and their own gut emotional reactions. This is not to suggest that preschoolers are unaware of or insensitive to their brothers' or sisters' problems. It simply indicates that the intensity and range of emotions that siblings feel toward one another dur-

ing their early childhoods is not yet measurably or consistently affected by the children's illness or disability.

WATCHING YOUNG SIBLINGS TOGETHER

Interviews can provide us with rich information about what children feel and think. However, they do not provide information about what children do and how they actually behave. Only through direct observation of the children together can such information be obtained. Through the use of videotapes, the interactions between brothers and sisters have been recorded and analyzed. Most of this work, to date, involves observations of siblings of children with developmental, as opposed to medical, problems.

When the behavior of children with mental retardation and their brothers and sisters is compared to the behavior of other pairs of brothers and sisters, some very interesting similarities and differences are found. In a series of observational studies, Stoneman, Brody, Davis, and Crapps (1987, 1988, 1989) videotaped children with mental retardation and nondisabled children, ages 4–8 years old with their older brothers and sisters (ages 6–12 years). They reported that there were no differences in the emotional quality of the interactions between the two groups of siblings. There were no differences in the amount of affection or aggression expressed by the children. As compared to siblings of children of normal intelligence, siblings of children with mental retardation more readily assumed the role of manager or caregiver for their brothers and sisters. This was especially the case with older sisters. They also found, in later interviews with the children and their parents, that older sisters of children with mental retardation babysat and had more childcare responsibilities than any other group of brothers or sisters. The more family responsibilities that the siblings assumed, the less they participated in their own activities outside of their homes, and the more conflict was found in their relationship with the child with mental retardation.

Brothers and sisters (ages 1–11 years) of children with Down syndrome (ages 1–10 years) were observed and compared to other sibling pairs of similar age and background in a study conducted in Canada (Abramovitch, Stanhope, Pepler, & Corter, 1987). They found that brothers and sisters of children with Down syndrome assumed the dominant leadership roles usually seen among older siblings. Thus, even though some of the children were younger than their brother or sister with mental retardation, they behaved as though they were older. Though the two groups of siblings were viewed as very similar in the nature of their interactions, siblings of children with Down syndrome showed significantly more nurturing and affectionate behavior toward their brothers and sisters than other siblings of typical children.

Young siblings of children who are either handicapped or non-handicapped, ages 3 to 7 years of age, were observed playing together in their homes with and without their mothers present (Lobato, Miller, Barbour, & Hall, in press). There were no differences between the sibling groups in the amount of affection or aggression the children displayed with each other. However, interesting differences between the groups occurred within the mothers' behavior toward the children. Specifically, mothers were more demanding and scolding of sisters of children with handicaps than any other child, even though the sisters' behavior was not observably different.

UNIQUE EXPERIENCES OF YOUNG SIBLINGS

Though young siblings seem to share similar feelings and interactions with their brothers and sisters with handicaps or chronic illnesses as other children do with their healthy brothers and sisters, there are some stressful experiences unique to their situations that cannot be ignored. These experiences and concerns are outlined in Table 2.2 and discussed below.

As discussed in the latter section, siblings' general description of their feelings toward their brothers and sisters do not often include mention of the child's illness or disability, though they usually recognize that the child has special problems and acknowledge that

Table 2.2.   Unique concerns for young siblings

Confusion about the child's developmental or medical problem
Misconceptions of the cause of the problem
Emotional distress among parents and other family members
Disruptions in plans and family routines
Prolonged and frequent absence of the child and parents
Frequent medical and therapy appointments
Heightened attention to the child
Comparisons of health and development

there are more disruptions in their family plans and routines. However, young siblings do not always understand why these events happen or how they are related. Some of the difficulty during this early period stems from young siblings' immature understanding of the problems with which their brothers, sisters, and parents are trying to deal. Additionally, preschool- and kindergarten-age children have emotional and physical needs of their own that require a good amount of parental attention and energy. Often it is difficult to balance their normal needs with those of a child with a significant medical or developmental problem. Let us take some time now to examine young siblings' unique sources of stress.

Young Siblings' Concepts of Medical and Developmental Problems

The understanding that young siblings have of their brothers' or sisters' problems represents a unique blend of what they have been told, overheard, observed, and conjured up on their very own. Even though each child is unique, there are marked similarities in the ways in which different children at the same stage of development conceive diseases and disabilities. It is also true that as children mature, their understanding of these problems change and mature as well. Children under the age of 8 years typically understand their world in terms of their own immediate observations and experiences. They have limited ability to abstract or think beyond their own experience and generally relate to events on the basis of one characteristic at a time. They have a very vague, often "magical," understanding of cause and effect, and have difficulty understanding how entities that they cannot physically see or feel could cause something concrete to happen. This type of egocentric, concrete thinking lends itself to certain ways of understanding and misunderstanding disabilities and illnesses.

First, children understand disorders in vague, general terms. They tend to focus on one or two functional aspects of the disorder at a time. They do not retain a great deal of detail about specific symptoms (Bibace & Walsh, 1980; Burbach & Peterson, 1986; Potter & Roberts, 1984). For example, a child may insist that he or she

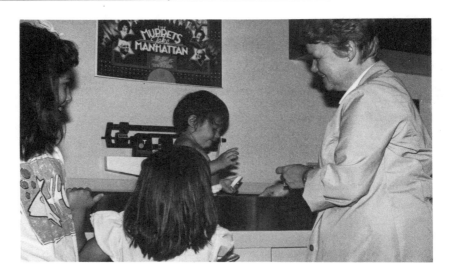

knows all about the brother's or sister's cerebral palsy being the reason why he or she needs a wheel chair but then turns around and asks why he or she can't use a spoon.

Young children are very vulnerable to the concept of contagion (Burbach & Peterson, 1986; Potter & Roberts, 1984). They are much more likely than older children and adults to think that they will "catch" almost any disease or disorder if they come close to the person who has it or go to the areas where that person has been. Part of the reason why youngsters are confused about contagiousness is because they do not fully understand what actually causes most conditions. Common misconceptions about the cause of the problem reflect youngsters' self-centered and concrete thinking. They often believe that something they did caused the problem. For example, one young 6-year-old boy remembered his pregnant mother reprimanding him for leaving a drumstick on the floor. This caused his mother to slip and say something to the effect of, "If you keep leaving your toys around and Mommy falls, the baby could get hurt!" Though the incident really had nothing to do with his sister's meningitis at a few weeks of age, the boy believed it had. Young children are more likely than others to blame themselves for an illness and to believe that "being sick" is a punishment of misbehavior (Perrin & Gerrity, 1981). In general, if you ask preschoolers the question, "Why do children get sick?" many of them will answer, "Because they are bad" (Perrin & Gerrity, 1981).

Children confuse the cause, effect, and treatment of a problem and do not readily differentiate between them. Take, for example, the 4-year-old girl defining her brother's mental retardation as meaning, "He has to go on a different bus in the morning." "Handicapped" means "you have a special place to park your car in front of buildings" and "leukemia" means "you have to go to the hospital and can't go to school." One young boy informed his teacher that his brother "got diabetes because he was sick."

Young children are very much influenced by what they can see. This makes it easier to accept that a child truly is ill or has a problem if there are visible manifestations of the problem. Physical symptoms can help justify why another child receives differential attention and treatment. Contradictorily, being able to see the problem makes it difficult for the youngster to understand diseases or disabilities that are not visible. In these cases, the child "doesn't look sick" yet parents and others certainly treat them differently.

While many siblings will answer, "I don't know," when asked what words such as "cystic fibrosis," "handicapped," or "leukemia" mean, there are others who divulge a level of understanding and compassion well beyond their years. The dialogue below took place with a 5-year-old girl whose 1-year-old brother had multiple medical and developmental problems at birth. We were enacting a scene with dolls in which I played the role of a little girl who asks her friend questions about handicaps. (This role-play interview technique is described in detail in Chapter 8.)

Adult: *Janie, I have some questions I want to ask you. The other day I was sitting at home with my mother and my mother told me that some new little boy moved into our neighborhood. And that this little boy has a handicap.*

Child: *Oh, that's too bad. I hope he feels better some day.*

Adult: *Well, I don't really understand what it means to have a handicap. Could you explain it?*

Child: *Well, a handicap is something, like, uh, you know my*

My brother Johnny has down Syndrome. A down Syndrome person is regular. Everybody has 20 Cromisones in there body and down Syndrome children have 21. They are Special. It is a Merical that I have a brother like John.

Nicole
Grade 2 Age 7

brother? He's in a wheelchair. Well, that's something like a handicap.

Adult: *Well, what else?*

Child: *It means sometimes you have crutches or sometimes braces or sometimes you have a handicap like, uh, you're on a respirator or something like a machine.*

Adult: *What kinds of things can handicapped children do?*

Child: *Well, sometimes they grow up and learn how to, uh, like uh, well, just play "one potato, two potato." Sometimes their arm . . . one arm is weak and one arm is really good and they can rattle something or something like that.*

Adult: *Uh-huh. Well, are handicapped children happy or are they sad?*

Child: *Sometimes they're sad and they feel bad, but, and sometimes if they have a brother or if they have a . . . or they, they have a sister, well . . . uh . . . they, uh . . .* (Loses train of thought). *What did I just say?*

Adult: *You said, sometimes if they have a brother or if they have a sister . . . .*

Child: *They, um, they, the brother or sister feel bad.*

Adult: *Why do they feel bad?*

Child: *Because their brother or sister is handicapped and they don't know if they're gonna grow up not to be handicapped or grow up to be handicapped.*

Adult: *Oh, now I understand more. Thank you very much for telling me. I really did want to know because that was a word that I had never heard before.*

Though this 5-year-old girl is rare in her wisdom, she captures the emotions and concerns that many siblings eventually come to experience at some point during their childhoods. They come to understand disabilities and illnesses as problems that affect their brothers, sisters, and themselves. While siblings maintain hope for the child's future, they really don't know what to expect. And though the child may have a problem, siblings often find ways of discovering the child's strengths and playing together as children.

Special Problems within the Family

Once it is clear that young siblings do not always understand why the events surrounding a child's illness or disability occur, it is easier to realize how they can be confused by some of the other special concerns listed in Table 2.2.

There is generally considerable emotional distress among the adult members of the family around the time that the child's illness or disability is being identified by the family and diagnosed by professionals. If the child who is impaired is younger, older siblings will observe and experience the changes in their parents' behavior. However, if they are still young children themselves, they will have difficulty understanding these changes. Young children are vulnerable to believing that their own behavior is the cause for their parents' distress. Young siblings may try, through their own behavior, to relieve their parents' sadness. For example, a 5-year-old girl made her mother and father a beautiful valentine and promised to be very good so that they could be happy again. Not only is a young child vulnerable to his or her parents' feelings of sadness, but siblings may also feel sadness about their brother's or sister's condition as well. Even if it is a newborn brother or sister whom the child has not yet even met, siblings may experience sadness or loss in regard to the little companion of their imaginations.

Many parents report that their routines as a family are very much affected by a child's illness or disability. Plans they make must involve considerations for the child's health and ability. Plans commonly must be adjusted due to unexpected fluctuations in the child's status. Similarly, new activities become part of the family routine, such as visits to and by professionals. These all become part of the siblings' lives as well. While siblings who come along after an older child's handicap has been identified readily accept these aspects of their family as "the way it's always been," other siblings, who knew life before the child's illness or disability, often are aware of the changes in their family's activities and mood. Older siblings not only must adjust as all earlierborns do to the arrival of a new sibling, but they also have the additional challenges of heightened attention to that child's special needs.

One other special consideration for young siblings that bears mentioning is that of the comparison of the health and development of siblings. It is a quite common practice for parents to compare their children to one another. It is also common for siblings to do the same. When one child is ill or has a developmental problem, a young sibling may actively look for similarities and differences between his or her own status and that of the other child in order to determine whether or not they are well and able themselves. When the sibling is younger, to an older child who has significant developmental delays or functional restrictions, the comparison can be a bittersweet experience. While the younger sibling may feel relief and appreciation of his or her own health and abilities, he or she may feel some confusion, guilt, or sadness in surpassing what the older siblings can accomplish. Some children respond to this temporarily by diminishing or concealing their own strengths and activities. For the older child with the handicap, seeing his or her younger sibling surpass him or her in skill and/or liberties is a sobering experience, as well. While the child may be sincerely pleased that his or her sibling is not affected, the younger sibling serves as a regular reminder of his or her problem.

Many preschool-age children "try on" some of the unique behaviors of their brother or sister who is handicapped. Much of this "trying on" simply reflects the enormous amount of imitation that takes place between young siblings. The experimentation with illness or disability behaviors is usually very temporary and can actually help the young siblings realize that one of the differences between them and the other child is that they exercise some control over the symptoms. Of course, if the young sibling gains inordinate attention for these behaviors as compared to other more appropriate behaviors, an undesirable pattern of somatic complaints can be encouraged (e.g., "All you have to do to get attention around here is act crazy or get sick!").

SUMMARY

While young siblings are usually aware of the functional aspects of a child's illness or disability, they do not always understand it. There is wide variation among young siblings in what they actually know about their own brothers' or sisters' problems. Some children know next to nothing at all, while others show extraordinary wisdom and sensitivity.

Despite these differences in knowledge, when children are young, their experiences with and feelings toward their brothers and sisters are much the same, regardless of the conditions of the child's health or development. They can experience love, affection, hostility, and aggression. However, in time, the affection and companionship they feel can be colored with a sense of pride for the child's accomplishments, worry about the child's future, and responsibility for the child's care. They come to understand that a disability or illness not only affects a child, but everyone in the child's family, including themselves.

CHAPTER 3

PSYCHOLOGICAL ADJUSTMENT OF BROTHERS AND SISTERS

GIVEN THE IMPORTANCE AND EMOTIONAL RICHNESS OF sibling relationships, it is not unreasonable to question whether or not children's psychological adjustment will be affected in significant ways when one of their brothers or sisters has a chronic illness or developmental disability. The purpose of this chapter is to examine the effects of the child's problems on important aspects of sibling psychological adjustment. While many authors state strong opinions about the possible psychological effects of a disability or illness on siblings, relatively few can substantiate their claims with convincing data. In the discussion that follows, only the more sound research projects are reviewed.

Most research studies deal with the emotional and behavioral adaptations of siblings with particular types of disorders and diagnoses. For this reason, the discussion that follows is organized according to the types of disabilities or illnesses that are involved. As will be discussed later, though, the actual diagnosis of the child usually has relatively little effect on siblings' psychological adjustment.

ADJUSTMENT AND DIAGNOSIS

The following types of disabilities and illnesses are discussed in this section: mental retardation, physical disabilities, severe learning and behavior disorders, developmental disabilities, and chronic medical illnesses such as diabetes, juvenile rheumatoid arthritis, and leukemia.

Mental Retardation

The term mental retardation is one used when a child's intellectual and independent living skills are very significantly below what would be expected of a child of the same age and culture. The causes of mental retardation are many, and can include chromosomal abnormalities such as Down syndrome as well as social-environmental deprivation. While children who have mild mental retardation do not excel academically in school, they can often work and live independently in the community as adults, or require minimal assistance to do so. Contradictorily, children with severe or profound mental retardation often have other associated physical handicaps and require intensive special education and assistance in all aspects of their daily living throughout their lives. Thus, the effect of the child's needs on the family may vary greatly from one family to the next, even though the children share the same diagnosis.

One of the first controlled studies of siblings examined the adjustment of 83 college students who had brothers and sisters with varying degrees of mental retardation (Grossman, 1972). They were compared to a group of 66 college students whose brothers and sisters were of normal intelligence. The groups of siblings were similar in terms of their academic year level; family social and economic status; number, birth order, and gender of the brothers and sisters; and their religious affiliations. All of the college students participated in a standard interview designed to assess their psychological adjustment in four areas: academic achievement, overall academic functioning (including social adaptation), intelligence, and anxiety levels. There were no significant differences between siblings of children with mental retardation and nonhandicapped children. In fact, siblings of children with mental retardation received higher scores on measures of overall college functioning. The author considered the possibility that the siblings who participated in the project may have been more open and better adjusted than most siblings of children with mental retardation in the general population. The author assumed that siblings with negative feelings would be less interested in recounting them in an interview. While that may be so, the same argument also can be applied to those students whose brothers and sisters were of normal intelligence. Thus, in terms of overall adjustment, as adults, few differences between siblings of children with mental retardation and nonhandicapped children were uncovered. The differences that were identified favored the brothers and sisters of the children with mental retardation.

Siblings of children with Down syndrome (i.e., a chromosome abnormality that causes mental retardation) have received considerable attention in England by Ann Gath and her colleagues (Gath, 1972, 1973, 1974; Gath & Gumley, 1987). In the first reported study, Gath (1972) compared ratings from parents and teachers of the behavior of three groups of children. The first group consisted of 36 school-age siblings of children with Down syndrome. The second group included 35 siblings of children with cleft lip or cleft palate, and the third group consisted of children whose brothers and sisters had no known birth defect. The groups of children were similar in terms of their age, gender, and birth order. Their families were similar in size and general socio-economic conditions. The parents and teachers provided standard ratings of the children's behavior with peers and adults. No significant differences were found in the reported behavior of the siblings of the children with mental retardation and normal intelligence.

In a later investigation, Gath (1974) looked at a group of 174 children who had brothers and sisters with Down syndrome. The siblings ranged in age from 5 to 19 years and were compared to a group of children of similar age. However, there was no attempt to match the groups on some of the other important family characteristics such as size and birth order. In general, the groups were rated similarly on measures of psychological adjustment problems. However, sisters of children with Down syndrome were rated as having more difficulty getting along with other children and were considered by their teachers as being more antisocial than the sisters of children who did not have Down syndrome.

Siblings of children with Down syndrome were included in another, well-controlled study of psychological adjustment and behavior problems (Gath & Gumley, 1987). The children participating included 95 siblings of children with Down syndrome and 88 siblings of children with mental retardation not caused by Down syndrome. The siblings averaged 10 to 11 years of age. They were compared to 183 of their classmates who were siblings of children of normal intelligence. Brothers and sisters of children with Down syndrome were no different from the comparison group in their teachers' ratings of their behavior and social adjustment with other children and adults outside the family. Unlike the previous study (Gath, 1974), sisters did not exhibit any more adjustment problems than other groups of children.

Gruszka (1988) completed a comparison study of sibling adjustment, using 45 siblings of children with mental retardation of various causes and degrees and 45 siblings of children of normal

intelligence. Siblings in each group ranged in age from 3 to 17 years and were matched on the following characteristics: birth order, age, and sex of the children; number of parents in the home; and family socio-economic conditions. Mothers in both groups completed a standard questionnaire rating their nonhandicapped children's behavior problems and social competence. Social competence or ability is indicated by aspects such as the number of friends and frequency of contact with them, number of chores, and amount of participation in social activities outside the home. The children themselves completed a standard assessment of their own self concepts. The two groups of children did not differ in their mothers' ratings of their social competence or number and type of behavior problems. Furthermore, the children manifested similar positive perceptions of their own cognitive and physical attributes as well as their relationships with their mothers and peers. In other words, the way that the children felt about themselves and the way they thought others felt about them was not influenced by the presence of a brother or sister with mental retardation. Their thoughts and feelings about themselves and their families were similar to those held by other children their own age.

Physical Disabilities

Children can have a variety of physical disabilities; however, for the purpose of this section, only spina bifida, cerebral palsy, and multiple handicaps are addressed.

Children who have spina bifida, a defect of the spinal cord and spinal column, can exhibit a wide range of motor, intellectual, and behavioral skills, depending on the severity of the spinal cord defect. Some children have difficulty with bowel and bladder control, require the use of a wheelchair for mobility, and encounter significant learning disabilities in school. Other children experience numbness in their lower bodies but are able to walk without any special assistance and encounter minimal difficulties in school. Despite the numerous medical and educational problems that these children can experience, there is inconclusive evidence as to whether or not their brothers and sisters are generally negatively or positively affected.

In 1973, Tew and Laurence reported the results of their study of 59 British children with spina bifida and their 44 siblings, and 59 matched comparison children and their 63 siblings. The children ranged in age from 2 to 15 years. Tew and Laurence reported that siblings of children with spina bifida were almost four times more likely to show evidence of psychological maladjustment than the siblings of nonhandicapped children, as reported by their teachers.

The possible effects of spina bifida on siblings' self-concepts was examined in a study of American children between the ages of 8 and 9 years (Kazak & Clark, 1986). The children with spina bifida, their siblings, and their parents were very well-matched to a control group of families whose children all were developing normally. The siblings in both groups completed the Piers-Harris Self-Concept Scale. This is a questionnaire containing 80 items that children complete themselves via the paper and pencil format. The instrument measures children's overall self-concepts as well as their perspectives on their own happiness, popularity, level of anxiety, physical appearance, school performance, and behavioral functioning. Results indicated that there were no differences in self-concept between the groups of siblings. Brothers and sisters of children with spina bifida had a similar range of positive (and negative) comments to say about themselves. This is especially interesting since the parents of the children who had spina bifida reported significantly higher levels of stress associated with parenting a child with a handicap. Obviously, then, in the majority of cases, parents of children with spina bifida were managing their stress effectively enough to be able to provide an adequate emotional environment for the development of typical self-concepts in their healthy children.

In 1981, Breslau, Weitzman, and Messenger examined the psychological adjustment of 239 healthy siblings of children who had cystic fibrosis, cerebral palsy, myelodysplasia, and multiple handicapping conditions. The children ranged in age from 6 to 18 years and were compared to a group of 1,034 children "randomly selected" from New York City. No descriptive information regarding the comparison group is provided in the journal report, which suggests that important family factors such as marital status, socioeconomic conditions, and number of children were not controlled. Mothers provided information about their children's adjustment and the presence or absence of symptoms of the following types of psychological and behavioral problems: self-destructiveness, conflict with parents, anxiety, fighting, delinquency, and isolation. Results indicated that, as a group, siblings of children with handicaps and chronic illnesses did not differ from the other children in overall psychological adjustment. They were rated as having fewer isolation problems but more problems relating to fighting with peers and delinquency. The children were comparable in their reported self-destructive behaviors, conflict with parents, and levels of anxiety.

Severe Learning and Behavior Disorders

"Pervasive developmental disorder" and "autism" are diagnostic labels used for when children exhibit particular problems in the development of communication, social, and other intellectual abilities. Children with pervasive developmental disorders or autism frequently have mental retardation, and some can exhibit very unusual self-stimulating or self-abusive behaviors. Treatment generally includes intensive special education, behavior modification, communication training, and family support. Because so many aspects of the child's development are severely affected and because the management of the child's behavior disorder can be very taxing, the potential for negative effects on the child's parents and siblings is great. However, researchers have failed to find consistent differences between siblings of children with these disorders and other siblings of "normal" children.

Ferrari (1984) compared 48 children who had brothers who had been diagnosed as having pervasive developmental disorder or autism, diabetes, or normal, healthy development. The siblings were between the ages of 8 and 12 years and were matched to the comparison children on birth order, family size, socio-economic status, and marital status of the parents. The children responded to a standard self-concept questionnaire. Their parents completed a questionnaire rating the children's social competence and behavior problems. The children's teachers also rated them in terms of their self-assurance and confidence. Contrary to expectations, there were no significant differences between siblings of healthy and ill or disabled children on the child measure of self-concept. Teachers did not report the self-esteem of siblings of healthy children to be differ-

ent on the whole than the self-esteem of children whose brothers or sisters had autism or diabetes. In addition, there were no overall differences found between the groups of siblings when their parents' reports of the children's social competence were compared. In fact, parents of children with diabetes and developmental disabilities in this study tended to rate the healthy siblings as having greater involvement in social activities, though the difference was not statistically significant. Furthermore, there were no statistically significant overall differences between the groups of siblings of children who were healthy and those who were disabled in the number of behavior problems reported by their parents. Interestingly, siblings of children with pervasive developmental disorders were rated as having the fewest behavior problems of any group, while siblings of children with diabetes were rated as having the most behavior problems. Part of the reason why siblings of children with diabetes may have been rated as having more problems may have been that this diagnosis was made closer to the time of the study than the diagnosis of pervasive developmental disorder for the children in the other group. When the researcher statistically controlled for the effect of the amount of time since the diagnosis, the difference between the siblings of children with diabetes, developmental disorders, and normal children disappeared. Thus, even with a childhood condition as costly and poorly understood as autism or pervasive developmental disorder, these brothers and sisters appeared to be as well-adjusted psychologically as other groups of children.

Other Developmental Disabilities

Some researchers have not divided children with different developmental or medical diagnoses into separate groups, but have studied siblings of young children with a wide variety of significant developmental handicaps, as a whole, and compared them, as a group, to siblings of children with normal development (Dyson, 1989; Lobato et al., 1987, in press). Twenty-four youngsters, ages 3 to 7 years, who had brothers or sisters with significant handicapping conditions such as mental retardation, cerebral palsy, and spina bifida were compared to a group of children whose brothers and sisters were not known to have any developmental problems. The groups of children were matched on family size and income, sibling age, birth order, gender, age-spacing between the children, and marital status of their parents. Information obtained directly from testing and observing the children themselves revealed no differences between the two groups in terms of the children's self-esteem and their thoughts about their mothers' feelings toward them. Additionally, their behavior with their brothers and sisters was similar in nature.

However, the mothers rated the behavior of the two groups of children differently. Compared to mothers of nondisabled children, mothers of children with handicaps rated their "normal" sons as being more aggressive and depressed and their daughters as being more aggressive. Thus, even though the siblings of the children with handicaps were similar to other children their own age in terms of their self-esteem and behavior, their mothers expressed more concern about their behavior.

In another investigation of sibling self-concept, social competence, and behavior problems, Dyson (1989) compared 110 older siblings of young children under 7 years of age. The siblings ranged in age from 7 to 14 years. Half were siblings of children who were normal in their development and half were siblings of children who had a diagnosed developmental problem such as mental retardation, physical and sensory handicaps, learning and behavior disorders, and general developmental delays. The degree of severity of the disabilities ranged from mild to severe, according to parents' judgments. The families were similar to one another along important demographic lines. Overall, the siblings of the children with handicaps were not different from other siblings in terms of their self-concept, social competence, or number and severity of behavior problems. Siblings of children with handicaps, however, were less involved in extracurricular activities than other siblings. Evidently, though, this was not at the expense of their overall mental health and psychological adjustment.

Chronic Medical Illnesses

Most of the investigations of children whose brothers and sisters have chronic or terminal medical problems, such as juvenile rheumatoid arthritis, diabetes, gastrointestinal problems, cancer, cardiac problems, and cystic fibrosis, compare children from more than one diagnostic group within the same study. Because it would be cumbersome, and eventually repetitive, to describe them separately, each study (with its various diagnostic groups) is described below as a whole.

Rheumatoid arthritis is quite uncommon in children. Common symptoms include stiffness and pain in the joints, swelling and inflammation of the joints, fever, and a rash. Any joint can be affected though the neck, spine, ankles, knuckles, and wrists are more commonly involved. The effect of the disease varies greatly from one child to the next. The severity of the symptoms can vary from hardly noticeable to crippling. Some children occasionally will require aspirin to treat the illness, while others may require a wheelchair or other adaptive equipment to move around. Obviously, then, the range of effect of the disease on the child and family can vary as well.

Siblings of children with rheumatic disease have been studied by Daniels and her colleagues at Stanford University in Palo Alto, California (Daniels, Miller, Billings, & Moos, 1986; Daniels, Moos, Billings, & Miller, 1987). Mothers of 72 children with rheumatic disease and 60 healthy children completed a questionnaire indicating whether or not the siblings had psychological and behavioral problems (e.g., anxiety, feeling sad, having nightmares, discipline problems at school) and physical problems (e.g., allergies, anemia, asthma, colds, headaches, stomach aches). In addition, some children could be rated as having "multiproblems" that are simply a reflection of having numerous problems in both the psychological and physical domains. As a whole, the siblings of the children with rheumatic disease and good health were comparable in self-esteem, emotional and psychological adjustment, academic status, and peer relationships. In fact, siblings of children with rheumatic disease reported slightly higher numbers of family activities and greater social involvement in school. According to their mothers' reports, the groups of siblings were similar in the number of physical symptoms of illness; however, the siblings of children with rheumatic disease were more likely than comparison siblings to perceive themselves as having allergies and asthma.

In another investigation (Tritt & Esses, 1988), the self-concepts, behavioral adjustment, and anxiety levels of 10 siblings of children with juvenile rheumatoid arthritis were examined and compared to 11 siblings of children with diabetes and 6 siblings of youngsters with gastrointestinal problems. This group was then compared to a group similar in gender and age of the sibling, socio-economic status of the family, and employment status of the mother. The children were all around 12 years of age. Most of their brothers and sisters had been diagnosed as having their medical problems approximately 3½ years prior to the study. Results indicated that there were no significant differences in the self-concept and anxiety levels of the groups of children as measured by questionnaires completed by the children themselves. In contrast, mothers of children with chronic illnesses thought their "normal" siblings had more personality problems when compared to mothers of healthy children. However, they were judged by their mothers as having no more than the usual problems with conduct or immaturity.

LaVigne and Ryan (1979) studied the psychological and behavioral adjustment problems and the positive social characteristics of 57 siblings of children with significant cardiac problems (e.g., ventricular septal defect), 37 siblings of children being seen in a plastic surgery clinic because of visible physical deformities (e.g., cleft lip, cleft palate), and 62 siblings of children who had leukemia or other cancerous conditions. Their mothers completed a standard questionnaire, and their responses were compared to the mothers of 48 healthy control children. Unfortunately, the groups were different from one another in terms of the number of years of the fathers' and mothers' education and their income. The healthy families were highest in education and income, and the families of plastic surgery patients were the lowest in these areas. When one considers the lower level of medical bills experienced by the healthy families, the differences in expendable income between the groups of families were probably even greater than indicated. There were no significant differences among the four groups in the areas of: ages of the siblings, family size or number of children in the home, and marital status of the parents. Despite the difference in family education and income, generally there were no significant differences between siblings in the four illness groups and the comparison group. As a whole, siblings were rated similarly by their mothers in terms of aggression, sensitivity, fears, immaturity, social inhibition, academic or learning problems, and overall psychopathology. Thus, the fact that there was a child with a chronic illness, and, in some cases, terminal illness, in the home did not cause measurable psychological harm to brothers and sisters. Though the group as a whole was similar to other children of the same age, subgroups of siblings did have significantly more difficulty. According to their mothers' reports, preschool-age siblings of children with plastic surgery needs had more problems that related to social withdrawal. In all of these cases, the child patient had a visible defect and in the majority of the cases, the child had a facial anomaly such as a cleft lip or cleft palate. The authors of this study felt that the visibility of the child's problem was significant to the young, preschool-age sibling.

Siblings of children who have diabetes also have received some attention. As with almost all other chronic illnesses, the severity and effect of the diabetes can vary between individuals. Treatment of childhood diabetes often consists of daily injections of insulin, a diet low in concentrated sugar, regulation of physical exercise, and control of infection. As children with diabetes mature, responsibility for the injections and diet generally pass gradually from their parents to themselves. While children with diabetes may miss a considerable amount of school and may be restricted from some strenuous activities, they generally enjoy a similar variety of childhood experiences as their nondiabetic peers.

Ferrari (1984, 1987) reported two studies that included siblings of children with diabetes. As mentioned earlier, the first project involved the comparison of children whose brothers had pervasive developmental disorder, diabetes, and no medical or develop-

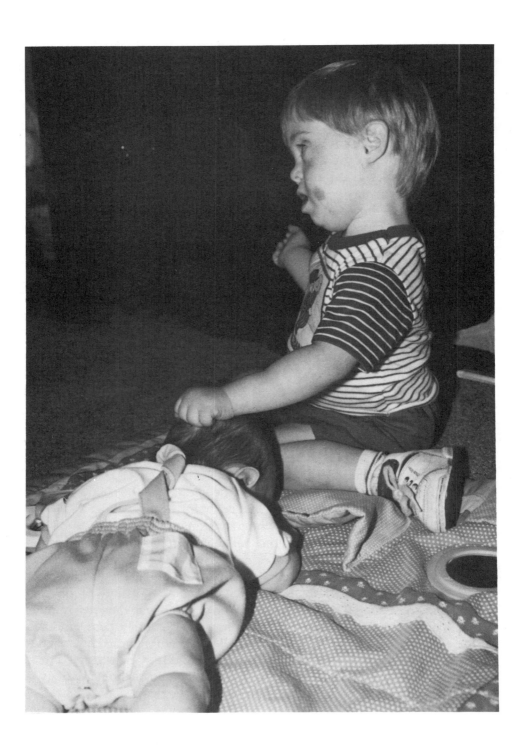

mental problems. There was a tendency for siblings of children with diabetes to have the highest level of reported behavior problems. Further analysis of the data, however, demonstrated that all of the increase in behavior problems among siblings of diabetic children may have been due to the fact that these families had more recently learned of their child's diabetic illness. Therefore, the families of children with diabetes may have been in the process of adjusting to their child's newly discovered medical needs. When the amount of time since the diagnosis of the disease was accounted for, the difference in reported behavior problems between the siblings of the children who were healthy, diabetic, and developmentally disordered disappeared. In contrast, siblings of children with diabetes showed higher levels of social competence than siblings of well children. Brothers of children with diabetes, however, rated themselves as the least happy or satisfied of all of the groups of children. However, there was a tendency for all brothers (regardless of health condition) to rate themselves as less happy and satisfied than sisters. Despite this negative tendency, there was a positive difference between the groups of siblings, in favor of the siblings of children with diabetes. Their mothers' reports of behavior with others at home and at school indicated greater social competence among the siblings of children with special needs.

In the second project reported by Ferrari (1987) presenting information about the self-concepts of siblings of children with diabetes, 60 children between the ages of 7 and 13 years completed a standard self-concept questionnaire. One-half of the children had brothers or sisters with diabetes, while the other one-half had brothers and sisters who were healthy. The groups were matched on important demographic variables. The results indicated that the two groups were basically similar in self-concept regarding their behavior, physical appearance, anxiety, and popularity. However, compared to other children, siblings of children with diabetes had lower overall self-concepts. They exhibited particular difficulties in self-concept related to their intellectual and school status and their happiness and life satisfaction. It is interesting to note that, similar to Ferrari's previous investigation (1984), brothers of boys who were diabetic had the lowest self-concept scores of any subgroup examined in the study. Thus, while siblings of children with diabetes appear to function adequately on the average, there are some siblings who report less happiness and satisfaction with life. Brothers, as opposed to sisters, appear to be the most vulnerable to these types of problems.

Cystic fibrosis is a chronic, inherited disease that affects the glands in the body that produce mucus. Abnormal mucus that is difficult for the body to expel, via its usual means, causes blockage in the child's lungs. This blockage can significantly impair breathing. In addition, the mucus blocks the pancreas and affects the child's ability to digest food. There is not yet a cure for cystic fibrosis but with modern treatments, most children live into their early adulthood. Management of the disease includes a regimen of special respiratory treatments, physical therapy, medications, and a special diet. Children require frequent doctor and therapist visits and, often, extended hospitalizations. The need for special family routines and adjustments is obvious.

Farkas (1974) conducted a comprehensive examination of the psychological adjustment of siblings of children with diabetes, mild cystic fibrosis, and cystic fibrosis in the terminal stages, as compared to siblings of healthy children. The psychological variables studied included anxiety, depression, guilt, personality adjustment, and the children's perspectives on the future. All of the information was obtained directly from the siblings themselves, rather than from their parents. There were no significant differences between any of the groups in their overall psychological adjustment, even among those children whose brothers and sisters were in the terminal stages of the cystic fibrosis. Similarly, Breslau and her colleagues (1981) found no significant differences between siblings of children with cystic fibrosis and siblings of children who were healthy and those who had other physical disabilities. In some cases, siblings of children with cystic fibrosis have better self-concepts than the average child (Gayton, Friedman, Tavormina, & Tucker, 1977).

SUMMARY

There has been a fairly widespread popular belief that siblings of children with disabilities and chronic illnesses have more problems in psychological adjustment than siblings of healthy, able children. Their problems have been attributed theoretically to assumed experiences such as parental neglect, guilt, shame, stigma, and extra childcare and household responsibilities, to name a few.

In general, review of the carefully controlled studies indicates that a child's disability or illness is not likely to have a negative effect on his or her sibling's self-concept, self-esteem, social competence, or behavioral adjustment. There simply is no uniform or direct relationship between a child's illness or disability and his or her brothers' and sisters' psychological adjustment. This is not to say that brothers and sisters are completely unaffected by an illness or disability. It simply suggests that they show no more evidence of major personality and behavior disorders than their peers. Siblings usually do have special concerns and feelings about their experiences with their brother or sister who is handicapped or chronically ill just as siblings have very intense positive and negative feelings about their healthy brothers and sisters. The research that is discussed in this chapter shows that it is quite uncommon for these special sibling concerns to translate into measurable psychological adjustment problems.

CHAPTER 4

INDIVIDUAL DIFFERENCES
WHY SOME SIBLINGS ADJUST
WELL AND OTHERS DO NOT

THOUGH IT IS NOT EXACTLY KNOWN WHAT DETERMINES A particular sibling's reactions, many characteristics of the child, family, society, and times in which they live may provide more information. In some cases, it might also be important to consider specific characteristics of the disease or disability as well. Examined here are many of these possible variables along with some of the evidence indicating the role that they may play in affecting the sibling of a child with chronic illness or disability. Many models for organizing these variables have been used in the past; however, a model that the author presented in one of her earliest papers on siblings (Lobato, 1983) is a relatively simple one to follow and has been adopted by others (e.g., Powell & Ogle, 1985). This model organizes all of the many factors that may affect a sibling's reactions into three major areas: characteristics of the child with a chronic illness or disability, characteristics of the siblings, and characteristics of the family as a whole. As may be noted, some variables seem like they could belong to more than one category. They are placed into only one category, however, for purposes of simplicity. (For readers who are interested in reviewing such models, the following publications are recommended: Crnic, Friedrich, & Greenberg, 1983; Crnic & Leconte, 1986; Drotar & Crawford, 1985; Lobato, 1983; Lobato, Faust, & Spirito, 1988; Powell & Ogle, 1985; Simeonsson & McHale, 1981.)

CHARACTERISTICS OF THE CHILD
WITH THE DISABILITY OR CHRONIC ILLNESS

Characteristics of the child with a handicap or chronic illness will be discussed first. As can be seen in Table 4.1, these characteristics include where the child lives, his or her gender, age, and the nature of the child's disease or disability.

Place of Residence

Prior to the 1970's in the United States, parents of children with mental retardation, multiple birth defects, or contagious illnesses were routinely offered the option of "placing the child" out of the home and into a residential care facility. Parents would often consider the "best interests" of their other children and the family as a whole in making this very difficult decision. Quite a bit of research

Table 4.1.   Characteristics of the child with handicap or chronic illness

Place of Residence
Gender
Age
Behavioral characteristics
Nature of the disease or disability
   Diagnosis
   Cause
   Prognosis
   Severity
   Onset

was conducted during the 1950s and the 1960s that examined how siblings psychologically adjusted to their brother's or sister's living at home or away from home. Knowingly, this research is now dated. It was conducted about 25 years ago, prior to the changes in general public awareness toward persons with disabilities and the development of community-based supports for the child and family.

While some of the information about sibling psychological adjustment during the 1950s and 1960s might be less relevant than it used to be, there are reasons why there are still lessons to be learned. As a society, we like to believe that all children today, regardless of their handicapping condition, are able to live at home with their families from birth; however, that is not always the case. There are still many families and communities who cannot rally the necessary resources—be they financial, emotional, or technological—to maintain their children safely at home (U.S. Department of Health and Human Services, 1988). Advances in medicine and technology have prolonged the lives of many children who, years ago, would have been lost, such as children born very prematurely and those who have suffered severe head or spinal cord injuries. However, the lives of some of these children are dependent upon highly sophisticated technical machines that, as yet, cannot be transported home. Thus, though the information is dated in some ways, the studies on the effects of residential placement are presented below, for the benefit of those who continue to face such decisions.

Farber and his colleagues (Farber, 1959, 1960, 1963; Farber, Jenne, & Toigo, 1960; Farber & Ryckman, 1965) conducted much of this early research. They looked at the effects of a child's mental retardation on the family by comparing those families whose children were raised at home with families who had placed their children in residential care. These projects did not include comparison families who did not have children with mental retardation. All of the reports dealing with sibling issues (Farber, 1959, 1960; Farber et al., 1960) indicated that siblings of children with milder levels of mental retardation were better adjusted (as rated by their mothers) than siblings of children with more severe mental retardation. Additionally, older sisters in families where the child with mental retardation remained at home had more difficulty than sisters of children raised outside of the home. The opposite was true for brothers. Boys tended to adjust better or have less conflict with their parents when the child with mental retardation lived at home. It is possible that sisters at that time often shared much of the childcare responsibility with their mothers, and, thus, were more likely to feel some of the negative effects of caring for a child who was severely handicapped at home.

These results have been replicated by others, though it should be kept in mind that the results are based on parents' reports during a time when children with mental retardation and their families had fewer community supports than are available today (Fotheringham, Skelton, & Hodinott, 1971; Fowle, 1968; Leanza, 1970). Collectively, those studies indicated that sisters, especially eldest ones who became very involved in the care of the child with severe mental retardation at home, were more likely to have psychological adjustment problems than other sisters.

Other projects (Caldwell & Guze, 1960; Graliker et al., 1962; Tew & Laurence, 1973) conducted at around the same time provided conflicting results and failed to support the conclusion that residential care of the child was better for siblings. In one of the projects (Caldwell & Guze, 1960), the researchers interviewed siblings of children with mental retardation themselves in addition to interviewing their mothers. One-half of the 32 families that participated had a child with mental retardation living in an institution, while the other one-half had all of their children at home. No differences or measures of anxiety and attitudes between the two groups of siblings were found during the interview. Siblings' attitudes and feelings toward the child and the reasons for his or her residential placement out of the home tended to parallel the opinions expressed by parents. The relationship between parents' and siblings' attitudes is important and will be explored in greater detail later.

Gender

Very few studies have actually tried to determine whether the gender of the child with a handicap or chronic illness has any effect on the psychological adjustment of his or her siblings. Because so little has been done, strong conclusions cannot be reached. The few existing published studies provide conflicting evidence. Siblings may have an easier time adjusting to a sister with diabetes than a brother with that illness (Ferrari, 1987), but adjust equally well to brothers and sisters with mental retardation (Gath & Gumley, 1987). Though

the gender of the child with the handicap is probably fairly unimportant, it is generally accepted that psychological adjustment among siblings may be better when the affected child is of the opposite gender (Ferrari, 1987; Gath & Gumley, 1987; Grossman, 1972). Siblings report more embarrassment from their brother or sister with a handicap when that child is of the same gender and of similar age (Grossman, 1972).

One of the major issues for siblings is to establish themselves as individuals with separate identities. This is true for all siblings, even those whose brothers and sisters are healthy and able (Bank & Kahn, 1982; Wagner, Schubert, & Schubert, 1979). When the child with the handicap and the sibling are of similar age and gender, they may enjoy the benefit of close companionship; however, this access and closeness can also provide more opportunity for conflict. The more similar siblings are in outward appearance (e.g., age, gender), the harder they probably will have to "work" in order to establish their separate identities.

Age

As a child with a chronic illness or developmental disability gets older, the needs of that child and the services available may change as well (Svelze & Keenan, 1981). In the case of progressive illnesses, the child's needs are going to increase with age. In the case of children with developmental disabilities, many parents report that their child's and family's isolation from others grows greater as he or she matures physically, but not mentally or socially. The difference between their child and others seems much more apparent when he or she is older. In the comprehensive study of the siblings of children with developmental disabilities, Dyson (1989) found that the siblings of older children showed slightly higher levels of adjustment problems.

Behavioral Characteristics

One last characteristic of the child with a disability or chronic illness that may be important for a sibling's development is that child's own level of social and behavioral adjustment. The results of most investigations indicate that though there are exceptions (Kazak & Clark, 1986), children who cope effectively with their disease or disability tend to have siblings who do so as well. Conversely, "affected" children with symptoms of poor adaptation (e.g., low self-concept, behavioral problems, chronic anxiety) are more likely to have siblings who exhibit the same characteristics (Cairns, Clark, Smith, & Lansky, 1979; Daniels et al., 1986, 1987; Gath & Gumley, 1987; Grossman, 1972).

Cairns and her colleagues (Cairns et al., 1979) described re-markable similarity between pediatric cancer patients and their healthy siblings in terms of self-concept, anxiety, and feelings of vul-nerability to illness and injury. Of children with rheumatic disease, those who show more psychological and physical problems have siblings with more problems as well (Daniels et al., 1987). Children with mental retardation who have behavioral problems at home are reported to have a more adverse effect on their mothers and siblings than children at similar levels of mental retardation who do not ex-hibit behavior problems (Gath, 1972, 1973; Gath & Gumley, 1987; Walker, Ortiz-Valdes, & Newbrough, 1989).

Reasons for the correlation between the psychological and be-havioral adaptation of a child with a disability and that of the well-sibling are explored in a later section.

Nature of the Illness or Disability

It is widely accepted that different illnesses and disabilities can have different effects on the day-to-day lives and futures of children and their families. It is equally true that the daily functioning of different children with the same diagnosis can be very different. Examined below is whether or not certain characteristics of the disease or dis-ability have any effect on sibling adjustment.

Diagnosis The diagnosis a child carries appears to bear little relationship to a sibling's adjustment to disease or disability.

Dyson's study (1989) of 55 siblings of younger children with handicaps indicates that siblings of children with mental retardation have fewer behavioral problems, higher self-concepts, and greater social competence than siblings of children with physical or sensory impairments, speech disorders, learning and behavioral disorders, and developmental delays. It is somewhat difficult to interpret this aspect of Dyson's data, however, since she did not clarify how chil-dren were classified into these general handicap categories. One might assume, for example, that children considered to have "men-tal retardation" showed significantly slower development than chil-dren described as having "developmental delay"; however, this is not explained.

When Gath and Gumley (1987) compared siblings of children with Down syndrome (that usually results in at least moderate men-tal retardation) to siblings of children with mild mental retardation of a nonspecific cause, they found a higher rate of adjustment and be-havioral problems among the latter group. Siblings of children with Down syndrome had fewer behavioral problems and were doing much better in school than siblings of children with nonspecified mild mental retardation. It is important to note that mild mental re-tardation is associated much more frequently with lower socio-economic, educational, and intellectual functioning in parents (Robinson & Robinson, 1976). There were more adverse social conditions among these families in Gath and Gumley's study that may have partially accounted for why the siblings of children with mild mental retardation were particularly poorly adjusted.

Cause or Etiology It is important to consider the cause of a child's developmental or medical problem when considering its effects on siblings. If the "affected" child's problems are at least partially attributed to adverse environmental conditions that are shared by the siblings, then adverse effects on the siblings can be expected, as well. In such a case, the sibling's psychological problems should not be interpreted as caused by the "affected" child's disability or disease. The problems experienced by both children could be attributed to the negative aspects of the environment that they share. Similarly, as siblings share the same gene pool, they may inherit the same vulnerabilities to illnesses and disabilities. In these cases, difficulties experienced by the sibling may reflect a milder form of expression of the "affected" child's problems. For example, siblings of children with diagnosed autism (i.e., associated with severe language problems) are more likely to have mild language and other learning disabilities themselves (August, Stewart, & Tsai, 1981). It would not be appropriate to attribute these difficulties solely to the experience of being raised with a brother or sister with autism since both children may share a constitutional predisposition to language and learning problems.

Prognosis The prognosis for a child refers to the expected course and outcome for the child in the future. Is the child (and family) to face progressive decline with early death, or a regular life expectancy with unpredictable periods of dysfunction or illness? The process of coping with different future outlooks varies; however, no consistent association with major aspects of the well-siblings' psychological functioning have been identified. Even when siblings facing fatal illnesses were compared to siblings challenged with problems that were not life-threatening, their own self-concepts and measured behavioral and personality characteristics were similar (Farkas, 1974; LaVigne & Ryan, 1979). Though their day-to-day thoughts, feelings, and worries may be affected by the child's prognosis, the siblings' psychological foundation probably will not be directly affected.

Severity As is known, the same illness or disability can vary in severity from one child to the next. Many researchers have examined whether or not the severity of a child's problem influences a sibling's adaptation and development. As with most illness characteristics, there is conflicting evidence. Some researchers have found that the severity of disability or illness bears no direct relationship to sibling functioning (Breslau et al., 1981; Farkas, 1974; Grossman, 1972), while others have found differences between siblings grouped according to the severity of their brother's or sister's problems (Farber, 1959, 1960, 1963; Farber et al., 1960; Tew & Laurence, 1973). The fact that there is such conflicting evidence suggests that severity alone probably accounts for a small part of the picture. It is likely that the severity of a child's needs becomes important to a sibling's functioning when considered in conjunction with other characteristics of the sibling and family. For example, siblings in families with very limited financial and social means are more adversely affected when a child's illness or disability is severe and creates greater dependence (Grossman, 1972). Presumably, families who have fewer financial resources will not as easily be able to obtain help or respite. Thus, the substantial burden of the child's disability will have to be taken on by members of the family. Siblings whose parents hire outside help are less likely to be affected by the level of their brother's or sister's dependence and needs since the extra care is being shared outside the family.

    Onset   The time of onset, or when an illness or disability is detected, may have an important role in sibling adjustment. Young children whose older brothers or sisters have always had a problem are likely to have different perspectives than children who experience the stress and turmoil surrounding the diagnosis of a chronic illness or disability. Generally there is intense emotional and behavioral instability immediately surrounding a diagnosis or new loss of function (Harris, 1983; Wikler, 1986; Wikler, Wasow, & Hatfield, 1981). Siblings who are able to recall the time of a child's birth or diagnosis remember it as a time of great confusion, sorrow, and unpredictable behavior, especially in their parents. Some siblings have described that period of "initial" upheaval as lasting as long as a full year, but that life settles into a more tolerable routine thereafter (Grossman, 1972). When Ferrari (1984) compared siblings of children with diabetes to siblings of children who were healthy or developmentally disabled, siblings of children whose diabetes had only recently been diagnosed were the ones experiencing the greatest number of problems. When Ferrari controlled the amount of time since the diagnosis, siblings of children with diabetes were similar to the others in psychological adaptation.

CHARACTERISTICS OF THE SIBLING AND SIBLING GROUP

Table 4.2 contains a list of characteristics of the nondisabled, or well, sibling that researchers have attempted to associate with sibling functioning. These factors include characteristics of siblings as indi-

Table 4.2.   Characteristics of the sibling or sibling group

Age
Gender
Birth order
Age-spacing
Number of children in the family

viduals (e.g., age, gender) as well as characteristics of the siblings relative to one another (e.g., birth order, age-spacing). The latter types of relationship factors often are referred to as "sibling constellation" variables.

Gender

By themselves, the individual sibling characteristics of gender and age are not uniformly associated with variations in sibling adjustment problems. Of the studies that have found differences in the adjustment of males and females to their brother's or sister's disability, the difference has been fairly consistently in favor of the females (Breslau et al., 1981; Ferrari, 1984, 1987; Kazak & Clark, 1986; LaVigne & Ryan, 1979). While sisters may generally seem better adjusted during childhood than brothers, as adults they may be more vulnerable to psychological adjustment problems such as anxiety and depression (Farber, 1960; Fowle, 1968). Most researchers accept that the siblings' gender should be considered in conjunction with birth order and the gender of the child with the handicap or chronic illness. For example, though males, in general, are more at risk for behavioral problems, older sisters, especially in low-income families, may be particularly overburdened and adversely affected by a child's illness or handicap (Breslau, 1982; Farber, 1959; Fowle, 1968).

Age

The age of the sibling sometimes affects how that child appears to be coping. Studies that find differences between young and older siblings usually find that the children in the older age ranges have the fewest psychological adjustment or behavioral problems (Ferrari, 1984, 1987; Gruszka, 1988; LaVigne & Ryan, 1979).

Reasons why younger, preschool- and kindergarten-age siblings are reported to experience more problems may include some of the factors that have already been discussed. First, due to their level of cognitive development and limitations in experience, they are less likely to understand the conditions surrounding the "affected" child's illness or disability. Second, their parents and the

child with the handicap are more likely to be young and, therefore, closer in time to the discovery and diagnosis of the handicap or illness. Thus, their parent's reports of more behavioral problems may reflect this period of greater emotional instability. Third, preschoolers and kindergartners may have fewer opportunities for establishing associations and friendships outside the family. Their happiness and satisfaction may be more exclusively dependent on family matters; whereas older, school-age children usually begin to develop interests and close relationships outside the family.

Sibling Constellation Factors

Of all the fixed, unchangeable factors that may mediate sibling functioning, sibling constellation variables such as age-spacing and birth order appear to play the strongest role in sibling adjustment. Age-spacing (i.e., the number of years between children) exerts a great influence on most children (Wagner et al., 1985). The closer in age two children are, the more similar they are likely to be in their interests, abilities, desires, and needs. This produces very fertile grounds for competition and rivalry. The farther apart the children are in age, the less likely they are to need or want the same things at the same time. It is not surprising, therefore, to find that reports of behavioral difficulties and other adjustment problems are lowest among siblings who are 3 or more years older or younger than the child with the chronic illness or disability. Both Breslau (1982) and Dyson (1989), whose studies cover a wide range of illnesses and disabilities, found fewer indications of adjustment problems as the difference in the siblings' ages increased.

When the child with the handicap or chronic illness is older than a sibling by 3 or even more years, parents and other family members may have already made some of those critical early adjustments to the child's problem. When the next sibling comes along, special education or other day services may already be in place, providing an opportunity for the new sibling to receive a fair share of attention. When the sibling is older than the child with the handicap or illness by a few years, he or she will have had some time to get established and to develop prior to the new child's arrival. If the sibling is of school age, his or her relationships with others outside the home probably provide a form of buffer and support as events surrounding the younger, "affected" child unfold.

Where within the sibling constellation the child with the handicap or chronic illness appears has been an important finding in some studies when considered in conjunction with sibling gender. Those investigators who have identified differences in sibling adjustment according to the child's birth order and gender, generally find that the children who are more vulnerable to problems are older sisters and younger brothers (Breslau, 1982; Gath, 1972). However, birth order alone exerts relatively little control over a sibling's psychological adjustment to his or her brother's or sister's illness or disability (Ferrari, 1984, 1987; Kazak & Clark, 1986; LaVigne & Ryan, 1979; Tew & Laurence, 1973).

The number of children in the family has consistently been found to be important to sibling adjustment (Dyson, 1989; Grossman, 1972; Kazak & Clark, 1986). The greater the number of siblings, the better their psychological adjustment. Siblings who have at least one healthy, able sibling in addition to the child with the disability or illness have been judged as having more social competence and fewer behavioral problems.

There are probably a few reasons why children with more than one brother or sister adjust better. Simply having another family member available to help when assistance is needed can reduce the emotional and physical burden on all family members. Having a ready-made companion and confidante can also help a sibling through times when parents need to attend closely to the child who is disabled or chronically ill. When a child has another brother or sister to spend time with and to rely on, he or she is less likely to be as affected by changes in his or her parents' attention. In addition, having another well-sibling provides a child with a frame of reference for interpreting the experience of having a brother or sister with a disability or chronic illness. It appears that siblings in today's "larger" families of three or more children are most likely to develop the characteristics of tolerance and understanding that are admired.

CHARACTERISTICS OF PARENTS AND FAMILIES AS A WHOLE

Each of the characteristics of the siblings and the child with the disability or illness discussed above makes a small contribution to sibling psychological adjustment. Those factors that reflect more closely the conditions of the family as a whole (e.g., number of children, age-spacing) seem to play the largest role in mediating the effect of a child's illness or disability on siblings.

The characteristics of parents and families that are considered in this section include the facts regarding income and education levels, as well as those fluid, difficult-to-measure characteristics that reflect parent attitudes and stress, coping, and adaptation. These complex factors are listed in Table 4.3 and are explored below.

A family's socio-economic status reflects what the parents have achieved in terms of education, employment, and income. Socio-economic factors also reflect the type and amount of external resources that a family has access to when a problem arises. How-

Table 4.3.   Characteristics of parents and families

Socio-economic factors
Income
Parent education
Parent physical health
Parent psychological adjustment
Marital satisfaction
Family social support network
Family interaction and adaptation
    Communicativeness
    Flexibility
    Closeness
    Openness
    Expectations

ever, a family's socio-economics do not directly reflect other psychological or social resources of its members. When a family has the ability to arrange for outside assistance—either with childcare or household responsibilities—then one source of stress associated with significant illness or disability is alleviated. Parents, as well as siblings, can be relieved by sharing some of the day-to-day, emotionally and physically draining responsibilities (Grossman, 1972; Gruszka, 1988). However, exactly how a family is going to make the psychological and day-to-day adjustments to a child's illness or handicap is not closely associated with the family's socio-economic status. In most studies, socio-economic status is not as important as other aspects of family functioning in determining sibling adjustment (Daniels et al., 1986, 1987; Dyson, 1989; Ferrari, 1984, 1987).

Parents' physical and psychological health plays an important role in how their children, able or not, develop and adjust in life. A few projects have compared the psychological adjustment of siblings whose mothers did and did not have significant mental or physical problems of their own. Based on studies of mothers of children with rheumatic disease (Daniels et al., 1986), diabetes and pervasive developmental disorder (Ferrari, 1984), and spina bifida (Kazak & Clark, 1986; Tew & Laurence, 1973), it appears clear that a mother's own adjustment is critical to siblings. Mothers who report symptoms of depression and physical fatigue are the ones whose children also exhibit more problems with self-concept and behavior at home and at school. In fact, a mother's mental and physical health is probably more important in determining sibling adjustment than the presence or absence of the child with the handicap or chronic illness in the home. In other words, if a child has only healthy, able brothers and sisters, but has a mother who is depressed or in poor health, that child is at much greater risk for adjustment problems than the child who has a sibling who is disabled or ill but a mother who is healthy and basically happy.

When brothers and sisters describe their own experiences, they consistently emphasize the importance of their parents' reactions, level of acceptance, and adjustment (Gogan & Slavin, 1981; Grossman, 1972; Hayden, 1974; Klein, 1972; McHale, Sloan, & Simeonson, 1986; Sullivan, 1979; Townes & Wold, 1977). Young children model their behavior and develop attitudes in response to the behavior and attitudes that they experience on a daily basis through the important people in their lives. If the mood or behavior of their mother and father is generally positive and warm, then these feelings become part of the child's own experience. If, however, the parents are bitter and depressed, and approach the special needs of the child only with resentment, then these negative feelings are experienced by all of the children in the family. If parents (or others) attribute all of the family's problems to the child's handicap or illness, siblings are likely to do the same.

Aside from parents' individual attitudes or levels of adjustment, ways in which all family members get along are also factors. Instruments and questionnaires exist that measure the true substance of family living—how well members communicate, how affectionate and close they are, how flexible and tolerant they are, how much conflict they express, and how much time they spend together. Not surprisingly, a positive marriage, good communication between parents and children, and little conflict between family members predict good psychological adjustment for siblings (Daniels et al., 1986, 1987; Farkas, 1974; Ferrari, 1984; Gruszka, 1988; Kazak & Clark, 1986). Good communication and closeness in the family appear to provide the critical buffer between siblings and the added

stresses of having a brother or sister with a handicap or chronic illness. This pattern holds true even when families report that there
are significant stressors in the care of the special child (Kazak &
Clark, 1986). This suggests that families who talk about and try to
solve their problems together will create a better atmosphere for all
of their children.

Parents' attitudes and the family environment that they create
are clearly important for the psychological adjustment of the child
with the handicap or chronic illness as well. Children with developmental disabilities and chronic illnesses are more vulnerable to psychological distress and behavior management problems (Daniels et
al., 1987; Moos, 1984; Steinhausen, Schindler, & Stephan, 1983;
Walker et al., 1989). The child's adjustment is related not only to the
illness or disability but also to the parents' adjustment (Bedell, Giordani, Amour, Tavormina, & Boll, 1977; Hauser, Jacobson, Wertlieb,
Brink, & Wentworth, 1985). When both the child and the parents
experience psychological adjustment problems over time, siblings
may begin to show the same symptoms. When parents perceive
little support from their partner and/or others, they are more likely to
show significant signs of depression and fatigue that can translate
into problems for their children. In contrast, when parents feel a
good sense of support from one another and extended family and
friends, their own abilities to cope with distress are enhanced. The
benefits to all of their children are clear.

SUMMARY

Many characteristics of children, their illnesses and disabilities, and
their families are examined in order to understand why some siblings adjust well and others do not. When siblings are young, they
are less able to understand the conditions surrounding a brother's or
sister's problems. Their parents are more likely to be in a time of
crisis and emotional instability. Young siblings have fewer social
connections outside the family and are more likely to be sensitive to
the family problems than older children. To many parents of young
children, it may seem as though the child's illness or disability will
do nothing but harm to the other children. However, this is actually
quite far from the truth. As young siblings mature, evidence is clear
that they usually do not have more problems than other children. In
fact, many siblings show areas of great social and psychological
strength. Their relationships with and behavior toward one another
also tend to be more nurturing and positive than between many
other sibling pairs.

Sibling constellation factors and characteristics of an illness or
disability seem to play some role in sibling adjustment. However,

research suggests that other characteristics of the family—the way people feel about one another and cope with stress—are the ones that play a major role in sibling adjustment. Siblings do best psychologically when their parents communicate their expectations and feelings openly, talk about the illness or disability honestly, do not overburden them with childcare and household responsibility, and manage to maintain pleasant and supportive marital relationships. While these family styles of coping do not make the sadness of a child's illness or disability disappear, they do seem to enable brothers and sisters to develop some of life's most admirable personal qualities.

CHAPTER 5

SERVICES FOR
BROTHERS AND SISTERS

DURING THE LAST TWO DECADES, CHANGES IN LEGISLATION and public awareness have resulted in profound changes in the types of services available to parents of children with developmental disabilities and chronic illnesses. Theoretically, parents have become equal partners in the assessment and treatment of their own children. Parents have been entrusted with complex medical and technical information. They have become skilled therapists and nurses for their children, especially during the early years when the child is very young and receiving home-based early intervention services. Then, as their children get older, parents often take on the new role of special education advocate. With this new role comes the need for new information about special education regulations and procedures. Through their participation in the development of their children's Individualized Family Service Plans (IFSPs) and Individualized Education Programs (IEPs), parents can learn about new assessment techniques, the roles and contributions of various professionals to the care of their children, and the intervention techniques that are designed to promote their children's growth. Though these changes in laws and attitudes have brought a unique burden of responsibility to parents, in many communities there also has been a dramatic increase in the availability of parent support and training programs. The benefits of parent group support, discussion, and sharing of information and experience has been widely acknowledged (Abidin, 1980; Gabel, McDowell, & Cerreto, 1983; Harris, 1983). Parents' needs for support and training have become so accepted that it is hard to imagine a modern children's service that does not offer a range of parent activities.

Though these advances have been made in parent services, similar services for siblings are not yet routinely available. Only since the late 1980s has there even been appreciation of the fact that brothers and sisters may share some of the same needs for information and support that are experienced by their parents (Lobato, 1983, 1985; Powell & Ogle, 1985). With the advent of Public Law 99-457, professionals increasingly will be expected to provide services to young children with handicaps or chronic illnesses that address their needs within their family system. Inevitably they will become more familiar with the concerns of all family members. Hopefully, this will promote a broader range of services for brothers and sisters.

The purpose of this chapter is to review the special needs that siblings have that parents and professionals can work together to address. The different types of interventions that have already been described in the sibling literature are also presented. With each description is a discussion of the possible advantages and disadvantages of each type of program. It is important to note at the outset that only a minority of interventions have been conducted with very young siblings. Furthermore, few interventions related to medical problems have been described. The vast majority of programs focus on siblings of children with developmental problems; however, given the similarity in their needs, the information truly applies to both groups.

SIBLING NEEDS

Each sibling of a child with a handicap or chronic illness is unique. However, many of them share similar needs and concerns. While these needs and concerns change with age and circumstance, most siblings agree that they needed the following during their childhoods:

1. Information on the child's condition, including how it is evaluated and treated
2. Open communication within the family about the problem and family members' positive and negative experiences with it
3. Recognition by parents of the siblings' own strengths and accomplishments
4. Need for "quality time" with their parents on an individual basis
5. Contact and support from other siblings and families
6. Ways to cope with stressful events such as peer and public reaction, unexpected disruptions to family plans, and extra home responsibility

SIBLING DISCUSSION GROUPS

By far the most common type of program available for siblings is the discussion and workshop group. Perhaps discussion groups are popular because they are able to meet multiple needs simultaneously and to more than one child and family at a time. Sibling discussion groups can be effective in many important ways. First, they provide a forum for the exchange of factual information about disabilities and illnesses and their cause, assessment, and treatment. Secondly, they provide a rich opportunity for emotional support and development. Sibling groups tend to vary in their emphasis upon information versus emotional support and expression; however, all groups, by their nature, provide opportunities for both.

Groups that are planned as a sort of one-shot-deal usually focus most on providing information about disabilities and disease along with some structured discussion about the personal experiences of having a brother or sister who is handicapped or chronically ill. Though much can be accomplished on an emotional level, even during a one-shot-deal, this may not give all children sufficient time to develop the kind of trust in other group members that would facilitate heart-to-heart discussion of their deepest concerns and joys. Groups that begin with a plan to meet for an extended period are probably more likely to be able to address those emotional needs. However, even when the focus of the meetings is to share information regarding a particular diagnosis, the process of doing this with other children can create an atmosphere of peer understanding and compassion that can outlast the actual meeting time.

Discussion groups afford the opportunity to meet with other children in similar family situations and to share their unique and common experiences (Benson, 1982; Feigon, 1980; Lobato, 1985). Children can learn through their group that their family is not the only unique one. The group format gives the children the opportunity to explain the nature of their own family situation under relatively safe, nonstigmatizing conditions. Furthermore, it allows the children to hear people their own age describe and define various disabilities or diagnoses in terms that they can easily understand. In addition, the children can be exposed to common street terms that other children occasionally use to describe children with differences. By hearing and discussing these terms in the supportive environment of the sibling group, the children can begin to become less sensitive to them, and, perhaps, learn some new ways of coping with the rude and offensive language that they are likely to hear at some point in their lives.

In addition to presentations and discussions, another way in which children can acquire concrete information about and familiarity with various handicapping conditions and illnesses during sibling groups is to include observations and tours of the brothers' and sisters' special education or medical treatment facilities (Byrnes & Love, 1983; Weinrott, 1974). By observing and handling a range of assessment and treatment equipment pertinent to their own and other children's brothers and sisters, siblings can gain greater perspective on their own family member's experiences, strengths, and weaknesses.

In some cases, sibling groups meet separately from, though parallel to, ongoing parent discussion groups. In only a few published cases have meetings between parent and sibling groups together been described (Fairfield, 1983; Weinrott, 1974). While siblings are much more likely to feel at ease discussing their families without their parents being present, occasional, joint meetings can offer the opportunity to facilitate communication and understanding between the generations.

Parents whose youngsters have participated in sibling groups have reported that the experience made it easier for them to discuss their child's handicap or diagnosis at home. For some families, it is difficult to know when the nondisabled sibling is ready for conversation about a child's handicap. This often is the case when the child with the handicap or illness is older than the healthy children or when the children are very close together in age. By participating in a group, the children often go home talking about conversations that they had or comments that other siblings made about their own brothers and sisters. The child's own comfort in talking about these disabilities and illnesses can provide a strong signal to parents that this is a topic that is open for discussion.

Though difficult to measure, one of the major benefits to intervening with young preschool and kindergarten-age siblings is the opportunity it provides to contribute positively to the developing attitudes and behavior of the entire family. It is often during the family's early years, when the sibling or the child with the handicap or chronic illness is young, that parents want to know how their situation is likely to affect all of their children. A family's adaptation and communication patterns can be set early. By intervening and supporting everyone when their children are young, families can have the time to make the changes that might benefit their children in the long run.

Groups during the Preschool and Early Childhood Years

One of the earliest descriptions of the use of sibling groups appeared in the late 1960s (Kaplan & Colombatto, 1966). This sibling group did not actually address specific issues regarding the experience of being the brother or sister of a child with a handicap. The program was designed for young children, ages 30 months to 60 months, whose brothers and sisters had mental retardation. The families of the ten children who participated were financially disadvantaged. The program was run through the local Head Start program, in collaboration with professional staff of the regional program serving children with mental retardation. The program began as an 8 week summer session but expanded to a full school year after its success and popularity. The children attended the program 5 days a week for half days. The program was guided by much the same curriculum as the traditional Head Start program. Children were involved in field trips and general enrichment activities. There was no specific attention focused on issues related to the brothers' or sisters' disability, though professional staff were trained to have a sensitive ear to any child verbalizing a concern. Kaplan and Colombatto (1966) reported that the children "never became sufficiently organized or verbal to participate in even rudimentary discussions" (p. 32). It is important to note that the children participating in this program had no prior structured preschool experience and were somewhat delayed in the development of their own language and behavioral skills. The experience of these authors suggests that the developmental characteristics of siblings should be considered when designing a sibling program. Furthermore, reliance solely on verbal discussion of the topic with preschoolers is unlikely to be adequate. Hands-on experience and materials are needed to focus the children's attention and comments.

In 1981, a different type of group experience for young siblings of children with handicaps was designed (Lobato, 1981). It was this experience and information that formed the basis of the structured workshop series for young siblings included in Chapter 7 of this book. In this first attempt, children between the ages of 3½ and 7 years met together for approximately 90 minutes a week for 6 consecutive weeks during the school year. The children met in groups of three. Activities were designed to teach them about developmental disabilities, to help them recognize their own personal strengths, to recognize the positive characteristics of their brother or sister who was handicapped and other family members, and to teach them ways of coping constructively with stressful family events. The workshops were quite successful in meeting these goals. The children enjoyed the blend of recreational and informational activities and parents were satisfied by being able to have their well-child participate in a special activity. Additionally, for a few of the children, participation in the workshops was associated with improvements in their interactions at home with their brothers and sisters who were handicapped.

Groups during the Middle Childhood Years

Most other groups for brothers and sisters have been organized for older children; however, Murphy, Pueschel, Duffy, and Brady (1976) convened groups of middle childhood-age siblings in single weekday sessions to learn about Down syndrome. These children were taught about chromosomes and met with professionals to learn about physical therapy exercises and learning characteristics of children with Down syndrome. In the context of these informational sessions the children spoke to each other about their feelings regarding their brother, sisters, and peers.

Benson (1982) described a series of 2-day workshops for sib-

lings ages 8–15 years. The siblings attended informational sessions on the first day of the weekend that explained the basic nature and causes of mental retardation. Discussion of personal experiences took place later in the day. The second day of the workshop was strictly recreational. Entire families joined together for food and fun, providing the siblings with the opportunity to spend time with one another's brothers and sisters. This combination of recreation and information seems to be a critical formula for many sibling programs. Meyer, Vadasy, and Fewell (1985) also developed a set of structured activities to encourage discussion among older children who have brothers and sisters with handicaps. Even these well-focused activities, which are designed to take place throughout a series of weeks or months, are conducted in the context of larger recreational outings.

Though sibling groups often receive overwhelming support from parents and siblings (at least before they become teenagers), it is not a simple task to evaluate all of the potential long- and short-term effects of such groups. It is encouraging, however, to be able to say that there is convincing positive documentation of the immediate benefits and satisfaction of participating in sibling groups, even at the preschool level (Lobato, 1985). Evidence that sibling groups have been harmful has not been reported. When looking back on their lives as children, adult siblings often report that it would have been helpful to meet other siblings when they were young. Organized sibling groups provide just that kind of help.

SIBLINGS AS TEACHERS AND THERAPISTS

In addition to becoming involved in information and support groups, the expanded role of siblings as teachers or therapists has also been explored by parents and professionals. Such experiences take advantage of the fact that instruction and caregiving are natural components of typical sibling relationships (Cicirelli, 1975), especially in the behavior of an older sibling directed toward a younger member of the family. While many older siblings of children with developmental disabilities regard improving their teaching ability as desirable and satisfying (Lobato & Tlaker, 1985; Schreibman, O'Neill, & Koegel, 1983; Weinrott, 1974), many professionals remain cautious about overemphasizing the caregiving and teaching aspects of the siblings' relationship. The potential for inducing resentment on the part of either child is the primary cause for their concern. Most of the studies using this type of sibling intervention provided evidence that the siblings who participated in the training effectively acquired the targeted teaching skills and reported that they enjoyed the responsibility and interaction with their brother or sister. However, in other studies of sibling adjustment and coping, when siblings were interviewed about their daily lives but were not provided specific training in how to teach the brother or sister with the handicap, the siblings frequently stated that one of the negative aspects of being raised with a child with a handicap is the extra caregiving burden (Grossman, 1972). It also stands as an area of concern for many parents that the needs of the child with the handicap are imposing excessive demands on the time and patience of the nonhandicapped siblings. In fact, resentment and bad feelings toward a brother or sister with a disability is highest when a sibling has a lot of childcare responsibility (Gruszka, 1988).

The question is then raised: Why is it that siblings who assume the extra explicit role of teacher and therapist report feeling satisfied rather than burdened by the responsibilities? One plausible explanation is that such intervention studies are relatively rare and that the children who participated were probably carefully selected and screened. Siblings who showed little interest in the project when it was proposed were not "forced" to participate. Therefore, the children who eventually participated may not be completely representative of the much larger number of siblings who have participated in the broad survey and interview studies. Another possible explanation for this discrepancy, however, is that learning how to interact more effectively with one's brother or sister can be emotionally satisfying. In many of the sibling survey and interview studies, siblings rate their desire for information highly so that they can be helpful to their brothers or sisters (Sullivan, 1979). Thus, it may be that the satisfaction of making a positive contribution to one's brother's or sister's development can outweigh the inconvenience of extra responsibility. In addition, it is quite possible that resentment brews in the situation where a sibling has extra childcare responsibilities but none of the extra training or support provided in the organized projects.

Despite the cautions that have been raised, it has been shown that even preschool-age siblings can positively influence the self-care, verbal, and social abilities of their brothers and sisters with the handicap (Bennet, 1973; Colletti & Harris, 1977; James & Egel, 1986; Miller & Cantwell, 1976; Powell, Salzberg, Rule, Levy, & Itzkowitz, 1983; Schreibman et al., 1983; Whitman & Lobato, 1983). Some examples of such positive influence are presented below.

In one project (Whitman & Lobato, 1983), preschool-age siblings were visited in their homes by a tutor who taught them some simple strategies for prompting and rewarding cooperative behavior in their younger brothers and sisters with the disability. These 4- and 5-year-old children selected the type of game that they wanted to teach to their brother or sister with the handicap from an array of developmentally appropriate options provided by the tutor and parent. Not only did the intervention result in an improvement in the way the children played together, but it also resulted in positive changes in the kinds of feelings and attitudes the siblings expressed to their mothers regarding the child with the handicap. In two similar studies, parents, rather than a home tutor, were taught how to teach their children with mental retardation to play with their siblings (Powell et al., 1983). Similarly, two sisters taught simple games and desired vocalizations to their third sister who was handicapped via the use of positive reinforcement for appropriate behavior and ignoring inappropriate behavior (Miller & Cantwell, 1976). In still another study, Bennet (1973) taught a girl who was just $4\frac{1}{2}$ years old to teach plurals to her 3-year-old sister who was hearing-impaired. Cash and Evans (1975) also taught general positive instructional techniques to three preschoolers who had younger brothers and sisters with mental retardation.

All of the programs of this nature that are described in the professional literature are characterized by very close monitoring and evaluation procedures, perhaps due to the worry about undesirable side effects. This intensity of treatment and evaluation require either a 1:1 ratio, or close to it, as well as frequent contact with the supervising therapist or teacher. These requirements may render the approach somewhat impractical for many, though aspects of the model may be successfully incorporated into general parent training programs. For example, it may be perfectly reasonable to encourage parents who are participating in behavior training programs to consider brothers' and sisters' relationships as possible targets of intervention.

FAMILY PROGRAMS OF BENEFIT TO SIBLINGS

The interventions discussed above have been designed to directly address specific needs of brothers and sisters. There are other types of programs for families that consider and address the needs of siblings even though siblings are not particularly singled out. Many agencies organize activities that encourage recreation and play within the whole family as well as with other families whose children have disabilities or chronic illnesses. Such activities can strengthen siblings' sense of fun and belongingness within the family as well as provide them with contact with other brothers and sisters. For example, the Let's Play to Grow program of the Joseph P. Kennedy, Jr. Foundation encourages child development and family unity through play and recreation. Parents are guided to incorporate creative play activities into their home routines that explicitly include nonhandicapped brothers and sisters. Furthermore, suggestions are offered as to how parents can manage all of their children together in play and what should be expected in terms of typical sibling relationships (Morris & Schulz, 1989). Families participating in this program generally meet on a monthly basis for group activities and games that actively involve all family members. Because the

context of these sibling activities is game-like and adapted to all of the children's needs, the risk is minimized that siblings will feel overburdened with caregiving or attention only to the child with disabilities.

In addition to benefitting from programs that emphasize recreation and fun for family members, siblings can benefit from their parents' use of such community support services as specialized respite care. One of the major reasons parents consider using respite care is that it can provide their nonhandicapped or healthy children with opportunities for undivided attention or access to events that are not easily accessible or enjoyed by the child with disabilities or chronic illness (Fewell & Vadasy, 1986).

SUMMARY

The needs of siblings of children with handicaps and chronic illnesses are appreciated more now than ever as services have become better integrated into the family, educational, and community settings. Professional literature points to children experiencing needs for factual information about disabilities and their implications, open communication within their families, as well as contact and support from peers in similar life circumstances.

Once appreciated, however, these special needs warrant attention. Discussion groups and informational workshops that have served the needs of parents for so long, have become the most accepted and available forum for siblings. While high-quality curriculum activities have been developed for siblings who are more than 7 or 8 years of age (e.g., Meyer et al., 1985), the needs of young, even preschool-age, siblings remain to be addressed.

CHAPTER 6

PLANNING
A WORKSHOP SERIES
FOR YOUNG SIBLINGS

THOUGH INTEREST IN ESTABLISHING SIBLING WORKSHOPS IS likely to abound, a successful program will not run on enthusiasm alone. An enjoyable and effective program will require careful planning, creativity, and flexibility. The purpose of this chapter is to outline and describe the significant practical considerations in designing and running a group for very young siblings of children with chronic medical illnesses or disabilities.

PARENT INVOLVEMENT

Sibling support or workshop groups remain a relatively rare offering, especially for very young children. For this reason, it will be necessary to conduct some preliminary work with parents and other family members prior to organizing a workshop program.

Generally, there is great enthusiasm on the part of parents to involve their nonhandicapped or healthy children in educational and support groups with other siblings of children with disabilities or chronic illnesses. Most parents appear to value the opportunity for their healthy children to speak to and share their experiences with other brothers and sisters. In fact, in a recent survey (Wilson et al., 1989), more than one-half of the parents and siblings of children with severe mental retardation thought they would join a sibling group if one were available. Perhaps based on their own worthwhile experiences with parent support groups, many parents recognize the satisfaction of meeting and talking with people in similar situations. Additionally, if parents perceive that their children will enjoy the activities (even if they do not learn anything), enrolling their healthy children in the program can be one way for parents to balance all the special activities and attention given to the child with the handicap or chronic illness now and through the years.

Some parents, however, may have doubts as to the benefits of enrolling their children in a sibling group. These doubts should be anticipated and addressed openly. Though this appears to be a very small minority, some parents are concerned that such a program will result in too much emphasis on the child's handicap or illness. When the siblings' relationship is already perceived by their parents as positive and loving, they may be fearful that a sibling group would alter the child's attitude toward his or her brother or sister. The concern is that the sibling could begin seeing his or her brother or sister exclusively in terms of the handicap or illness rather than as a regular brother or sister. One way of addressing this concern is to summarize for the parents the results of studies that document the potential benefits of sibling groups (Lobato, 1985), and to indicate that, to date, negative effects of sibling groups have not been described. It is important to note in this context that children's awareness of their brothers' or sisters' disability has not been associated with negative behavior or attitudes toward them (Wilson et al., 1989). In fact, evidence suggests that even children who have very realistic appraisals of the severity of their brothers' or sisters' problems still can value them and the time they spend together. By informing and involving parents, their concerns and any misconceptions can be discussed.

Conduct a Preliminary Parent Meeting

Information that a sibling program is being considered should be sent to individuals through the applicable parent organizations or service agencies. A simple memo can announce the intention to hold a planning meeting to discuss sibling issues and parents' interests and concerns. The announcement should clearly indicate the age ranges that the program will address so that only parents of children in those age groups attend. A brief return slip should be provided on the bottom of the flyer for those parents who wish information about the group but are unable to attend.

The purpose of the planning meeting should be to begin discussion of some of the special issues common to young siblings of children with disabilities and chronic illnesses and to provide a rationale for offering sibling services. The meeting should last approximately 1½ hours. Anyone who is likely to participate as a leader in the actual sibling groups should be available for parents to meet. Parents should be surveyed regarding their concerns for their own children and what they would like to see addressed by the sibling program. While it is impossible to predict exactly what will be accomplished during each minute of a sibling workshop series, an outline of general goals and objectives should be shared with parents. Modifications to meet their particular needs can be discussed. Parents can be offered the opportunity to review the specific activities in advance of enrolling their children in the program.

By the end of the preliminary planning meeting, each family that is interested in becoming involved in the sibling groups should provide information about their family's schedules and hours of availability. Additionally, they should provide information regarding their children's ages, gender, and handicapping conditions so that plans can be made regarding the make-up of the sibling group.

Conduct a Home Visit

At least one home visit should be conducted for about 1½ hours before the first group meeting. The purpose of the visit is to become acquainted with the child, his or her family, and their home surroundings, and to collect some basic information for the group.

It is important to be personally familiar with the handicapping condition or illness faced by the child's brother or sister in order to have a reality base for later group discussion. Knowing who the child with the handicap is and what he or she can and cannot do allows the siblings' comments to be interpreted appropriately. If the child has a condition with which you are unfamiliar, more should be learned about it. It will be hard to teach the siblings if clear understanding of the disability or illness is not at hand. Ask parents for copies of the child's most recent comprehensive evaluation and educational or service plan. Discuss how they have defined their child's illness or handicap to the sibling. Discuss the kinds of words that will be used to explain the child's handicap or illness. This will promote consistency between you and the family. For the same reasons, have parents share any techniques that they may use to structure or discipline their child. If any special techniques will be needed, they should be reviewed in advance.

Have each parent complete a brief questionnaire like the one presented in Figure 6.1. (You may create your own form modeled after this example, or permission is granted to copy this questionnaire directly from the book.) This will provide information regarding the child's favorite activities, hobbies, colors, television shows, and so forth. This information will be useful for planning individualized rewards and snacks for the workshop meetings. Information should always be obtained regarding any of the siblings' special medical conditions or allergies that may be confronted during the group meetings. If any evaluations of the program are to be conducted, some of these activities should be incorporated into this home visit (see Chapter 8 for details on program evaluation).

Although time will need to be spent with each child's parents during this home visit, the majority of the time should be provided to the siblings who will be enrolled in the group. Establish a special relationship by playing with the child's toys, looking at his or her room, going for brief walks, and so forth. Bring a camera on the home visit so that a photograph can be taken of the sibling alone and with his or her brothers and sisters. These photographs will then be used in one of the later workshop activities. Bring an interesting treat or trinket to leave with the child as a teaser of the great fun that lies ahead at the workshop.

INTAKE QUESTIONNAIRE

Date: _____

1. **General information**
   a. Child's name: _____
      Date of birth: _____ Age: _____
      Gender: _____
   b. Parent(s) name(s): _____
      Home address: _____
      _____
      Home telephone: _____
   c. Sibling(s) name(s): _____
      Date(s) of birth: _____ Age(s): _____
      Gender: _____
      Nature of handicap or illness: _____
      _____
      _____
   d. Other(s) living with family: _____
      _____
      Age and relation to child: _____
      _____

2. **Child's schedule**
   a. Please cross out, on the chart below, those times when your child would *not* be available for the sibling group meetings or for a home visit.

	M	Tu	W	Th	F
9–10 A.M.					
10–11 A.M.					
11 A.M.–12 P.M.					
12–1 P.M.					
1–2 P.M.					
2–3 P.M.					
3–4 P.M.					
4–5 P.M.					
5–6 P.M.					

   b. Does your child attend preschool or elementary school?
      Yes _____ No _____ If yes, what grade? _____
      How often? _____
      _____
      _____

   c. Are there any other special activities that your child is involved in outside of your home (e.g., art lessons, dance classes, religious instruction)?
      Yes _____ No _____ If yes, please list these briefly: _____
      _____
      _____

(continued)

Figure 6.1. Brief intake questionnaire to be filled out by the parents.

Figure 6.1. (*continued*)

3. **Child's understanding and contact with special needs**
   a. Have you discussed your child's disability or illness with your other child(ren)?
      Yes _____   No _____
      If yes, please answer the following questions:
      1. How old was your child when you first discussed special needs? _____
      2. How soon after you were aware of your child's problem did you talk with your other
         child(ren)? _____
         _____

      3. Please estimate how often you have discussed these issues with your child(ren)?
         Every day: _____
         1–2 times per week: _____
         1–2 times per month: _____
         1–2 times per year: _____
         Other: _____
         _____

      4. Are there any materials that you have found to be helpful to you in these discus-
         sions (e.g., books, pictures)? Yes _____   No _____
         If yes, please describe: _____
         _____

      5. Are there certain words you use to refer to your child's special needs when speaking
         with his or her sibling?
         Yes _____   No _____   Please list: _____
         _____

      6. Are there any words you try to avoid using?
         Yes _____   No _____   Please list: _____
         _____

   b. Please list the activities/games that your children enjoy together (even for a brief period
      of time): _____
      _____
      _____
      _____

   c. Please describe at least two events that have brought you concern or enjoyment about
      your child's adjustment to his brother's or sister's disability or illness: _____
      _____
      _____
      _____
      _____

4. **Parent interests**
   a. What are your reasons for enrolling your child in the sibling workshop group? _____
      _____
      _____
      _____
      _____
      _____

_____

(*continued*)

Figure 6.1. (*continued*)

   b. Do you have any doubts or concerns about enrolling your child in the workshop group? _____

_____

_____

_____

   c. Do you have any particular questions or topics that you want to be covered during the sibling groups? _____

_____

_____

_____

5. **Other information for planning group activities**

   a. What size tee-shirt does your child wear? _____

   b. Please provide a list of the following:

      1. Snacks/foods that your child who will be attending the program likes

5. **Other information for planning group activities**

   a. What size tee-shirt does your child wear? _____

   b. Please provide a list of the following:

      1. Snacks/foods that your child who will be attending the program likes (and you approve of) and dislikes (or you do not allow):

         Likes: _____

_____

_____

_____

_____

      2. Any food allergies: _____

_____

_____

_____

      3. Favorite activities/games/materials: _____

_____

_____

_____

      4. Favorite television shows: _____

_____

_____

_____

      5. Favorite colors: _____

_____

_____

_____

   c. Do you have any particular questions or topics that you want to be covered during the sibling groups? _____

_____

_____

_____

   d. Please provide any other information that you feel will help make this an enjoyable and educational experience for your child: _____

_____

_____

_____

COMPOSITION OF THE GROUPS

Workshop leaders and the grouping of the children should be considered when composing the participants of a workshop series.

Workshop Leaders

People with many different backgrounds can run effective sibling
groups. No one particular degree appears to be essential. Necessary
skills or characteristics include knowledge of the individual children
and their families, knowledge of relevant disabilities and illnesses,
and good child management ability. The latter includes that special
balance of creativity, enthusiasm, and structure. In the past, the
workshop series in Chapter 7 has been conducted by psychologists
and social workers with advanced degrees, adult siblings and parents, graduate students, nurses, and early childhood educators. It is
recommended that parents who become group leaders or assistants avoid participating in their own child's group. Having the parent of a child present may dilute the sense of team camaraderie that
the child establishes with the other children and might restrict his or
her freedom of expression with the other children.

Grouping Children

If a young siblings' group is being organized in an area with few people, then a group, based solely on compatible family schedules and
locations, will probably have to be formed. However, if there are
many children to be enrolled in multiple groups, the following
should be considered: number of children, gender of the children,
ages and abilities of the children, and handicapping and illness
conditions.

Number of Children   In general, young children are going to
require more supervision than children older than age 7 or 8 who
have had at least 2 years of formal education. A ratio of one group
leader to four children is desirable for preschoolers. If a leader assistant is available, the groups should be limited to eight children. Children of this age generally have short attention spans and limited verbal abilities. Activities should be able to be varied frequently without
compromising anyone's attention and interest. Similarly, you will
need to be able to hear and respond to children's comments in a
constructive way and to supply a dense schedule of praise and reinforcement. Problems that arise in the group and the family should
be able to be responded to quickly. It is important to get to know the
children and their families before the group begins. Such accomplishments are more difficult when the student-to-leader ratio is
high.

Gender of the Children   It is recommended that mixed gender groups be formed whenever possible. Though there are not studies to confirm this point, experience suggests that mixed gender groups provide for more varied perspectives and peer modeling.

Ages and Abilities of the Children   The workshop series presented in Chapter 7 is designed for children roughly between the ages of 3½ years and 8 years. Some degree of mix in the ages and abilities of the siblings is desirable for the purposes of peer modeling. Minimum requirements for the group include being able to verbally express one's ideas in simple terms and to stay with one activity for approximately 15 minutes. If a child does not possess these skills, it might be wise to postpone his or her enrollment in the group until the program is next offered. Furthermore, children between the ages of 7 and 8 occasionally perceive themselves as "too sophisticated" for some of the activities and techniques of these workshops, yet are not skilled enough for an older sibling group that is based more exclusively on discussion. These children can easily be incorporated into the young group with the distinctive status of leader assistants. Though this child cannot be used as a substitute for an adult assistant when planning the student-to-leader ratio, he or she occasionally can be assigned circumscribed roles such as helping the younger siblings with their work.

Handicapping or Illness Conditions   It is not always feasible or desirable to group siblings together based on the diagnosis or label carried by their brother or sister. There are advantages and disadvantages to grouping by diagnosis. Simply having the same diagnostic label does not mean that two children will have the same strengths and weaknesses or face the same challenges. When children have similar disabilities, their siblings' sense of isolation from peers can be reduced. They can learn that they are not alone, but are part of a special group of children with a shared common interest. Young children often respond to a diagnostic label as invariable, that the word "cancer," for example, means the same for everyone. Though the children will learn otherwise in the workshops, just hearing someone else say that his or her brother or sister has cancer can establish a basis for a strong emotional connection between the children, even if the characteristics and needs of the children with the illness turn out to be vastly different.

When siblings whose brothers and sisters have different diagnoses and disabilities are grouped together, the children seem more motivated as a group to learn about different handicapping or illness conditions. They can learn that the challenges and pleasures that they experience are not always specific to a child's problem, but may also be related to his or her own behavior and that of his or her family. Thus, it can be quite valuable to mix children without regard to the specific diagnostic label. It is prudent, however, to avoid

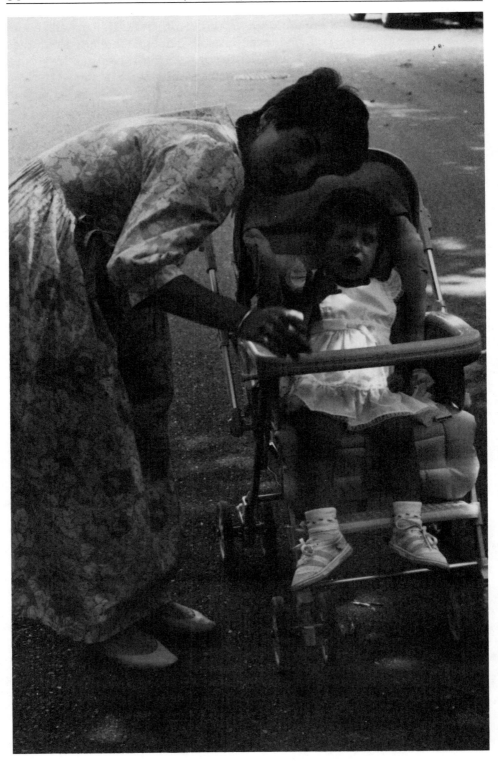

grouping together children whose brothers and sisters are at vastly different functional levels. When children whose brothers and sisters have severe impairments are grouped with siblings of children with mild, nonvisible difficulties, the children may perceive little ground of common experience. Though most siblings are understanding, to some, the concerns of the sibling with the brother or sister who is more mildly ill or handicapped may seem petty. Even though the psychological needs of such a sibling may be just as significant, it should be remembered that young children are greatly impressed by what they can actually see.

Brothers and sisters of children who are in the terminal stages of illness should be grouped separately from siblings of children whose disabilities or illnesses are chronic but not necessarily immediately life threatening. The activities included in this book do not address the needs that a sibling may have at the time of his or her brother's or sister's death.

WORKSHOP FORMAT

The format of the workshop should include some type of schedule of the program, the location of the event, the pace at which the workshop will proceed, and recommendations for the children's dress while attending.

Schedule of the Workshop

Early on, the number of sessions to be conducted during the workshop should be decided, as well as the length of the event. Though meeting once or twice a year can be useful for older, verbal children, its usefulness with children who are ages 3–8 is more questionable. The activities and information discussed at such workshops would be virtually meaningless since it would likely be so protracted from the children's ongoing lives. Though it can diffuse feelings of isolation, a one-time-meeting also might open wounds without the opportunity for healing. These potential disadvantages can be outweighed by greater parental involvement in a parallel sibling workshop, so that they can be the ones to pick up at home where the meetings leave off. Generally, however, it is recommended that the needs of very young siblings be addressed in a more ongoing, longitudinal fashion. The obvious disadvantage of ongoing groups is the staff's and families' commitment of time and resources. It usually is not possible for families to invest one day per month for years at a time into an ongoing group for siblings when the rest of their lives cannot be put on hold. Thus, a format that provides the benefit of some extended contact between children and staff, as well as a finite number of meetings, appears to be the most reasonable alternative.

The Sibling Workshop Series detailed in Chapter 7 involves six sessions of approximately 1½ hours each throughout the course of approximately 6 weeks. This level of program commitment means that the series can be offered on an annual or biannual basis, with different children rotating through at different times of the year.

Location of the Workshop

The most common site for the workshop groups described in the literature is at the service facility where the child with the handicap or chronic illness and his or her family receive treatment and assistance. For example, a private special education school, early intervention center, or hospital clinic can serve as the setting for the groups' meetings. Children whose brothers and sisters attend public schools are more likely to be spread around the school district. In those cases, common ground may be a classroom within the district. If no one location is suitable, consider the possibility of holding different meetings in different locations. While it generally is desirable to have one location, it is best to accommodate all that are involved. The advantage of one setting is that certain parts of the space for particular types of activities can be assigned. The children will come to associate certain areas with quieter, more reflective activities and behavior. This can assist in group behavior management. If a different location is chosen each time, not only will all of the workshop materials need to be transported, but the children will constantly have to adapt to new distractions.

Even when there is no obvious service facility or classroom, there are some reasonable options. Cooperative, though unrelated agencies, such as libraries, churches, and general daycare centers, may be interested in offering space as long as insurance liability and scheduling can be worked out. Another possibility to consider is rotating the group meeting through the homes of the participating children. One advantage of the home setting is that the siblings can more easily familiarize themselves with the home situations of the other brothers and sisters. However, the disadvantages of the family home probably outweigh the advantages. Most families do not have sufficient space for an extra eight or so children and adults. Those that do have enough space would have to shoulder an unequal extra burden. In homes, there are too many distractions caused by other children and adults, and the group itself can be completely disruptive to family members' routines. Additionally, the children who participate do not seem to appreciate the home environment as a very special setting for the program. It is the author's experience that the participating children's behavior is more conducive to discussion and concentration in a more clinical or school-like atmosphere.

Pacing of Workshop Activities

No young child should be expected to sit and listen to a lecture for 90 minutes or to work on only one project for that long. Therefore, it is essential that programs for young children keep a quick pace with much variation in materials that are presented and response-requirements. Activities that involve sitting still should be inter-mixed with those that allow movement. Alternate between thought-provoking activities and mindless fun. And remember, never have a meeting without a fantastic snack. Make use of local attractions such as zoos, farms, or ice cream stands for optional brief walks during planned breaktimes.

Dress Recommended for the Workshop

The children should be encouraged to dress casually, in comfortable clothing. A protective smock or over-shirt should be stored for each child. The activities will require children to be on the floor at times, so dress accordingly.

SUPPLIES FOR THE WORKSHOP

Supplies and materials necessary for the sibling workshops de-scribed in Chapter 7 are listed at the beginning of each workshop description. In addition to the specific materials listed, a broad selec-tion of preschool toys for the children should also be supplied for use during unstructured play periods. Arts and crafts that encourage self-expression (e.g., construction paper, crayons, paints, clay, markers) should be in plentiful supply. Hand puppets should also be abundant, one for each child and two for the instructors. Similarly, human figure dolls, toy houses, furniture, and neighborhood deco-rations such as flowers and trees will be needed.

Leader's Companion Packet

You may want to create a Leader's Companion Packet from a num-ber of the illustrations, photographs, activity forms, and evaluation forms that are shown in this book and are useful for implementing a sibling workshop. These might include: the Intake Questionnaire (pp. 79–81), the star chart (p. 89), the workshop photographs and illustrations (pp. 108, 109, 110, 112–113, 115–117, 128–131, 138–141, 144–145, and 149), the Parent Evaluation Questionnaire (pp. 158–159), the Sibling Activity Feedback Chart (p. 161), and the Sibling Workshop Evaluation Questionnaire (pp. 162–163).

Snack

An exciting early childhood program should offer fun snacks. Sometimes the ritual of food provides the atmosphere most conducive to thoughtful discussion. Parents may be interested in rotating responsibility for providing extra snacks; however, this responsibility should be on a voluntary basis. An inventory of any food preferences and allergies should be obtained prior to the group's meeting.

Rewards

Rewards can be offered the children for their appropriate behavior and their attendance and participation.

Appropriate Behavior   Children's participation in and cooperation with the group should be routinely rewarded through various means. Praise each child and the group, as a whole, lavishly and sincerely, using statements about the specific aspects of their performance that are valued. In addition, routinely use a star chart to indicate and reward instances when the children engage in verbal or nonverbal behaviors that are consistent with the goals of the workshop series. So, for example, if Mimi is requested to define a disability term and does so, she would receive a star. An example of a possible star chart appears in Figure 6.2. Occasions when it is particularly appropriate to use the star chart are indicated clearly in the workshop descriptions. Plan on preparing a new star chart for each meeting. A separate form of star chart may also be used on which the children may evaluate their enjoyment of the planned activities. The latter is described in Chapter 8, which focuses on program evaluation issues.

Participation and Attendance   Praise and star charts may keep the children enthused and focused during the meetings, thus increasing their participation. Their participation and enjoyment of the activities hopefully will also encourage them to return for subsequent meetings. Because continuity of attendance and participation is critical, consider a special reward that can be delivered in installments, contingent only upon the children's attendance, not their performance during the meetings. The children would receive a portion of their participation reward at the end of each session; thus, they will only be able to enjoy it and take it home when the workshop ends.

The following example of a participation reward is one that has been enjoyed by children who have participated in a previous workshop series. Buy simple colored tee-shirts in each child's favorite color along with iron-on letters of their names. At the end of each session, iron one letter of each child's name onto his or her shirt so that by the end of the workshop series, all children take home a shirt with their names on it as a memento. Do not allow the children to

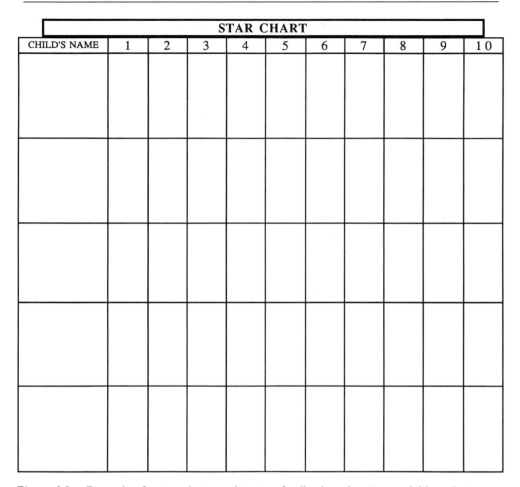

STAR CHART										
CHILD'S NAME	1	2	3	4	5	6	7	8	9	1 0

Figure 6.2. Example of a star chart used to give feedback and praise to children during a workshop.

take possession of the shirt during the weeks between the meetings. The only time that they should be allowed to see their prize is when a letter is being ironed on and at the very end of the workshop series.

SPECIAL EDUCATIONAL AND CLINICAL ISSUES

Some important special educational and clinical issues of which to be aware include: confidentiality, promoting generalization, techniques for encouraging group discussion, and program evaluation.

Confidentiality

When discussing young children, the word "confidentiality" takes on a unique meaning. One must remember that children at a young age do not have the same code of what is and is not a secret. As any preschool or kindergarten teacher will attest, children are likely to communicate "private" family matters to others. Thus, the siblings that participate in workshops are likely to go home and to talk to their parents, friends, and brothers and sisters about what was said in the group. Since you want to have a positive effect on family communication, the children should not be discouraged from talking to their own families about the other children and their families. Parents should also be reminded that their child may share information openly to the group.

The other aspect of confidentiality that must be considered is what will be done with the information that is obtained from the children. Will the parents be informed of everything that their children say? It would be appropriate to inform parents of how their child behaves during the group, and what he or she enjoys and appears to be learning; however, it would be inappropriate to tell parents exactly everything their child said, especially if taken out of context. Recommendations to them regarding the way they act or what they discuss at home, as well as questions or misconceptions that the child harbors, are all appropriate to share with parents. Children are not likely to share their thoughts and feelings with the group if they may come back to them in a punitive form via parents. If a child wants something to be a "secret" and keeping it quiet will bring no harm to the child or family, such a desire should be respected.

Promoting Generalization

As with any intervention, one's goal is to help children acquire new knowledge and skills that will be useful to them in real-life situations outside the confines and structure of the intervention setting. Though it can be very satisfying to a child to share one's joys and concerns with other youngsters, it is also a goal to enable children to discuss similar feelings with their families and neighborhood friends. Because sibling groups have not been widely available for young children, there are really no guaranteed techniques that can bring about generalization. However, experience to date, along with knowledge of how to promote generalization in other areas of learning, suggests certain steps that can be incorporated into the group sessions to improve chances that children and their families will benefit in a truly meaningful way as a function of their children's participation.

The first ingredient in promoting generalization is assuring that the content of the workshop discussion is relevant to the children and the families involved. After you have become more familiar with the children and the families who have enrolled for the workshops, review the activities of the sibling workshop series described in Chapter 7. Though these activities are applicable to a large variety of children and families, modifications can be made, if necessary, to

meet any individual needs. For example, if you believe that the children would benefit from reading a book about a particular disability or illness, however, one with a satisfactory narrative was unable to be located, consider modifying the words of an available text to better suit your needs. (This is especially easy to do when the children are not able to read yet.) Explanations of disorders and disabilities that are understandable to young children appear in Chapter 9. If no explanation is provided within Chapter 9 for a particular disorder with which a child in your group is faced, construct your own explanation. If modifications are made to the enclosed definitions or a new explanation is invented, it is advised that they be presented to other colleagues before using them with the children.

Another important way to ensure the relevance of the content of the workshop activities is to use the language and vocabulary that the children are most likely to encounter outside the group. The issue of labeling is a very sensitive one for most parents and professionals. Everyone is aware of the harsh words that some children and adults use to describe people with special needs. Such words can be painful to hear, especially when a child is young and the words are being applied to his or her own brother or sister. Because the words can be so hurtful, many parents and professionals choose to use only the most acceptable words when discussing a child's diagnosis with his or her sibling at home. The child is never exposed to the more pejorative language until he or she hears it from other children on the street. Many children in that situation find themselves very hurt and without a proper response or other way to cope with the pain. Similarly, there have been families that consistently used only a narrow range of technical terms to describe their infants' problems to their youngsters. Then, the children fail to recognize that people were talking about their own brother or sister when they hear less sophisticated "lay" terms to describe the infants' condition. For example, one family routinely described their baby as having a seizure disorder and never used words such as epilepsy, convulsions, or fits. When their 5-year-old daughter heard another child say that her brother had epilepsy, she became very upset, thinking that her brother had a second condition and that her parents had concealed this from her. Encourage parents to familiarize their children with all of the different words that may be used to describe a child's disability or illness. By exposing the children to the words in the safe settings of the home or workshop group, siblings may be more composed and capable of responding when they hear such words later.

Techniques for Encouraging Group Discussion

Because a primary goal of the workshops is to encourage open conversation and verbal expression of ideas and feelings, you need to be aware of techniques that will promote discussion between the children in the group. Whenever the children speak or ask a question, encourage them to ask their question to their peers rather than to the workshop leader. If they initially appear reluctant to do so, repeat or paraphrase to the group what the child has said so that the other children will come to understand that they are intended to listen. During the sessions, always praise children specifically for speaking directly to one another rather than through the leader (e.g., "Thank you, Rachel, for answering Joshua's question.") General questions should be answered this way, as well as questions that pertain to handicapping conditions or illnesses. For example, if Sarah asks, "What time will my mother come back?" a reply can be, "Gee, I bet the other kids might want to know when their mothers are coming back, too. Ask John or Heather if they know." If Sarah does not readily do so, then paraphrase her question to the group and encourage them to tell her directly by saying something like this, "Sarah wants to know what time her parents will be coming back. John or Heather, can you please tell Sarah when you think your parents will be coming back?" Similarly, if Joshua asks, "What does deaf mean?" turn the question over to the other children by saying, "That is a good question. I wonder if you can ask your friends here to see if any of them knows what deaf means?"

Throughout most of the workshops, questions for which there are no right or wrong answers will be asked. The goal will be to have the children raise as many issues and alternative solutions to problems as possible and then to discuss and evaluate them as a group. By consistently turning questions and answers over to the children themselves, they will be encouraged to express their ideas openly. In some instances, prior experience with the children may lead you to believe that none of them actually knows the correct information to a question of fact. This may make it difficult to turn the question over to them; however, resist your urge to answer before giving the children the opportunity to do so. Even if a few children answer the question incorrectly, this will provide you with a better understanding of what the children know and how they view their situations. You can then proceed with a more accurate answer to the question, incorporating into the response the new knowledge of the children's current level of understanding and vocabulary. If such a situation occurs, try to wind down the discussion by encouraging the original child who asked the question to summarize the new information for the group. For example, "Benjamin, now that we have talked a little more about sickle cell anemia, maybe you can tell Peter what it means." Give the other children the opportunity to elaborate on his answer. Throughout the descriptions of the workshop activities in Chapter 7, you will be prompted to specifically praise and reward verbal expression among the children. By setting an example of

good listening and clear speaking, the children will be encouraged to do the same.

Program Evaluation

Techniques for evaluating the effect of the workshop series are discussed in detail in Chapter 8. Review these carefully and plan evaluation activities prior to beginning the workshops.

SUMMARY

A successful sibling workshop program requires careful planning and consideration. Parent involvement is an important ingredient throughout. Workshop leaders are encouraged to become acquainted with siblings and their families via home visits, interviews, and questionnaires. When composing the participants of a workshop series, the ages, genders, and abilities of the particular siblings need to be considered, as well as the handicapping condition or illness of their brothers and sisters. A central location should be selected, preferably one associated with the care of the child with the illness or disability. Conducting the workshop will require a supply of a standard variety of preschool arts and crafts. In addition, you may also want to create and use a Leader's Companion Packet of illustrations, photographs, and forms from this book for implementing and evaluating the sibling workshops.

CHAPTER 7

WORKSHOP SERIES
FOR YOUNG SIBLINGS

THE ACTIVITIES DESCRIBED IN THIS CHAPTER ARE BASED ON numerous workshops that have been conducted with children whose brothers and sisters have faced a variety of medical and developmental challenges (Lobato, 1981, 1983). The workshops are designed for children between the ages of approximately 3½–8 years. Sessions are designed to last 1½–2 hours each and should be conducted during a period of 6–8 weeks. Each workshop in the series involves different activities for meeting specific goals. Activities are designed to build upon one another and should not be taken out of context. As a whole, the workshop series is designed to increase young siblings':

Understanding of developmental disabilities and chronic illnesses, in general

Understanding of the particular problem that their brothers and sisters face

Ability to identify and discuss the strengths of their brothers, sisters, and other family members

Ability to identify and describe their own personal strengths

Ability to identify and express positive emotions as they relate to family experiences

Ability to identify and discuss emotional reactions to stressful events related to their brothers' and sisters' disabilities or illnesses

Ability to generate alternative solutions for coping with difficult family experiences

Contact and discussion with other young siblings in similar family situations

Each workshop description includes a list of materials, many of which are readily available through stores that sell school supplies. In order to implement the curriculum as detailed, you may want to assemble a Leader's Companion Packet by copying photographs, illustrations, and other materials from this book (see p.87 for a suggested contents). Within each activity description are suggestions for how the activities can be explained to the children verbally. All suggested verbal presentations are accented in italic print. Each session also involves a group reading or storytime. The Annotated Bibliography contains a list of books suitable for young children. Books that are appropriate for your particular mix of children can be selected from this list.

FAMILIARIZING THE CHILDREN WITH THE WORKSHOP SETTING, FORMAT, AND RULES

GOALS

The goals of the first workshop are to familiarize the children with the setting, format, and rules of future workshops; to establish an atmosphere of camaraderie and support; and to encourage open discussion between the children. Much of the success of the series will depend on the children's experiences in this first session.

MATERIALS

The following is a list of materials to be used in this workshop:

Star chart
Easel
Decorative glitter
Quality puppets
Snacks
Safety pins
Adaptive equipment
Stickers
Construction paper
Safety scissors
Colored markers
Oaktag
Participation reward (part one)
Book for group reading

PREPARATION

Prior to the children's arrival, prepare a star chart (see p. 89 for an example) with each child's name in the column heading. Leave a margin in the left-hand column for listing behaviors for which the children will be rewarded with a star or sticker.

ACTIVITIES

There are seven activities in this workshop. They are titled: orientation, getting to know you, family drawings and discussion, snack, exploring adaptive equipment, group reading, and review, reward, and cheer. Approximate times to devote to each activity follow the title of the activity in parentheses.

Activity 1: Orientation (10 minutes)

This is the first meeting of your group—the one during which the children probably see one another for the first time and form their first impressions of the room and workshops. The children will check each other out and you should tour them through the various play and work spaces so that they feel as comfortable and at-ease as possible. As you guide children through the areas, point out to them the most fun aspects of the room (e.g., where the snacks are kept, where their own smocks and stickers will be stored, where you will sit altogether for stories and puppet shows).

After the initial tour around the room, bring the children together in a circle around an easel to make name tags. Using colored paper and markers, assist the children in writing their names and cutting out name tags. Pin them on their shirts and then go around the circle until each child can say the name of the others. Using the star chart, put a star or sticker on the chart for each child who can correctly name all the other children, including him- or herself, for laughs and guaranteed success.

Aside from learning one another's names, the children will also choose a name for themselves as a team. On the easel, list about three possible team names (e.g., The Sib Team, Brothers and Sisters Club, the Dinomite Kids) and allow the children to suggest other possibilities. Have them vote on what they want to call their team. Once decided, use their team name throughout the workshops whenever needed to give group instructions. But for now, you will help get the children excited about their special team memberships by leading them in a cheer.

Okay, "Sib Team." You know that all teams have cheers before their games? Well, we, the Sib Team, will have a cheer before our activities, when they're over, and before you go home. We will do the cheer, "Two-Four-Six-Eight" for the Sib Team. Does everybody know how to do that one? If someone does not know this cheer, teach it to him or her. *Okay, Team, huddle!* Have the kids huddle together, hand-in-hand in the middle of a close circle. In a loud voice, begin and get them to follow: *Two! Four! Six! Eight! Who do we appreciate? The Sib Team! The Sib Team! Yeah!*

Once the individual and team names are mastered, you should be ready to introduce the goals and rules of the sessions to the children. Words similar to the ones below have worked well and have been understood in the past:

You are all here today because you and your families are special. You all have brothers and sisters who need extra help in some way, like having to go to a lot of doctors or to a different kind of classroom or school. We are going to start meeting together so that you can talk to other children whose brothers and sisters have special needs. We will learn about those special needs and how different people and special equipment can be of help.

Each time we meet, I will plan special games and activities that will help us learn these things. Sometimes we will use puppets, build neighborhoods, and even draw and paint. After we finish those activities, you can have free play while I get your snacks ready. After snack, we will have other things to do like look at a piece of special equipment. Then we will read and talk a bit more about kids and families. After we are done reading a book, we will work on your special rewards. Do you know what special rewards you will get by the end of all the meetings? It is something we will put together a little at a time. It will be ready for you to take home only when all of our meetings are through.

Describe to and show the children the special rewards that you have designed for them for their attendance and participation in the workshop program.

Next, you will need to inform the children of the rules of conduct during the group meetings. Definitely discuss the limits of confidentiality as you have arranged with parents (see Chapter 6). Add any rules to the list below that you feel are important.

This is a place where we will talk about things that we think and feel and do. You can tell your Mom or Dad anything you want to about what we do and say here. I am sure that they want to hear what you tell them about our time together. But if you only want to talk about some things while we are here and not really talk about them at home, that will be okay because I won't be telling your Mom or Dad everything you say and do.

While we are together, there will be certain rules that we will all have to follow. Now pay attention to these rules because I'll be giving out stars for all of the rules that you can remember. Are you ready?

1. *We can talk in a regular voice like this while we are together but we cannot scream or yell unless we are doing our team cheer. There are other people in this building whom we should not bother.*
2. *If you want to play with the toys from the shelves, please ask me if you can use them before you get them. When you are finished playing with them, put them back where you got them.*
3. *If you want to use something that somebody else has, ask them if you can share it. Don't pull it or grab it away.*
4. *If you feel angry or bad about something that happens here,*

use your words to tell us what is bothering you so that we can help to make things better.

Ask the children to tell you the rules of conduct you just discussed. For each rule a child recalls, put a star next to his or her name on the star chart.

Activity 2:   Getting to Know You (10–15 minutes)

Your first goal will be to encourage the children to talk with one another about themselves and their family members. Review the suggestions regarding encouraging communication that appear in Chapters 6 and 9. Bring the children to the designated "quiet" or "reading" area of your space and have them sit on the floor in a small circle.

You will stage a puppet show about two characters, "Freddy" and "Darla" who are attending a playgroup for the first time. Select whatever names suit your group and stick to these names throughout the series. Freddy is shy and anxious at first, but gregarious, confident Darla will coach him into conversation and interaction with others. As the group leader, you will manipulate Freddy and Darla. Through the puppet show, Freddy and Darla will demonstrate the kinds of questions that children can ask in order to learn about each other. You will then give the children their own puppets in order to join in with Freddy and Darla in asking questions of one another. As the children become more comfortable talking with one another, you may find that they begin speaking more directly to each other and less indirectly through the pup-

pets. This is a desired outcome and should not be discouraged. Your puppet show should proceed similar to the scenario below:

Freddy (with eyes cast down, glancing briefly up to the children in circle): *Where are we? Who are all these kids? I wonder what they are doing here.*

Darla (upright and bold in her posture): *What kids?* (Looks around at group.) *Oh! Those kids! I think that they're here for the brothers' and sisters' group. But I'm not sure. If you want to know, you should ask them.*

Freddy: *I can't ask them. I don't know them. And since I don't know them, I can't talk to them.*

Darla: *Well, if you don't talk to them, you'll never know them. And then you'd have to spend all this time wondering who they are instead of becoming friends and playing together. What, are you shy or something?*

Freddy (looking down): *I don't know. I guess so. They look like fun kids who I'll want to be friends with but I just don't know what to say.*

Darla (confidently to Freddy): *Well, if that's the only problem, don't worry, I'll show you what to do. Watch me and listen to what I do. I'll start to find out who they are and where they come from. I don't think they come from Mars so I'm not scared.*

(to the children): *Does anybody here come from Mars?* (pause) *Phew!*

(to Freddy): *I'll start by telling them my name and then asking them their names.*

(to any individual child): *Hi! My name is Darla. What is your name?* (pause) *My friend, Freddy, here, feels a little shy right now but would like to learn more about you. Will you put on one of these puppets and help him out?* Allow the child to select a puppet from your collection.

(to child): *Now, you ask Freddy his name and where he lives.* Allow time for the child to ask the question and for Freddy to respond.

Freddy (to child): *What did you say your name is again? Do you know any of the names of the other children here? Yeah? Tell me one you can remember and let that child pick out a puppet, okay?* Allow time for a second child to select and put on a puppet.

Darla (to Freddy): *After you find out people's names you can ask them other things like how old they are and where they live.*

(to second child): *You ask her (the first child) some of these other questions to show Freddy what to do so that he can do it with someone else.* When the child finishes, have Darla praise him or her.

Darla (to Freddy): *Okay, now you make friends with someone else.*

(to group without puppets): *Raise your hand if you want to put on a puppet and talk to Freddy.* Give puppets to all the children who raise their hands.

(to Freddy): *They all look ready now. Can you think of what you might ask one of them?*

Freddy (confidently to one child): *Hi! I'm Freddy. What's your name? (Pause) How old are you? (pause) Where do you live? (pause) Do you go to school? (pause) What's your favorite toy? (pause)*

Darla (to group): *Hey, Freddy has the hang of it, but now he's hogging all the questions. Let's have you two* (pick any two children) *use your puppets to ask questions of each other like Freddy and I did. If you get stuck and can't think of a question or answer, maybe one of these other puppet people can help you out!*

Go around the circle so that each child has ample opportunity to tell very basic information about him- or herself. Put the puppets away when the kids are finished. Go over to their star charts and put a star next to each child's name, praising them for being such great talkers and helping out Freddy and Darla.

Activity 3:   Family Drawings and Discussion (30 minutes)

The purpose of this activity is to elicit conversation from the children about themselves and their families. Bring the children to the group table. On the table, have ready crayons, markers, colored pencils, and plain white drawing paper.

Tell the children that everyone is to draw a picture of their family, with all members of the household in it. The picture will be of their family doing something. The children will decide what the family will do together. If some of the children are from single-parent households, allow them to choose whether or not to include the out-of-home parent. However, if the child's brother or sister with the handicap or chronic illness lives outside the home, indicate that he or she needs to be included in the picture. Encourage the children to make this the best picture possible, to really take their time. As everyone draws, begin asking them questions about their drawings. Encourage the children to look at one another's work periodically as you ask questions. Don't forget to encourage questions and answers between the children themselves. Sequence your questions from the most neutral and general to more specific and individual to each family member. Usually one question and answer leads naturally to its own follow-up, but you might consider the series of questions below if the children need more concrete prompting:

Now, where is your family going to be in your picture, Chad?

Heather, what is your family doing? Is that something you like to do together a lot in real life?

Joshua, tell Pam about the garden and building you've drawn there.

Rachel, who in your family are you drawing now? Tell me about him or her. What does he or she like to do? What does he or she look like? What does he or she usually do with you on weekends? (Repeat variations of these for all family members.)

Give equal emphasis and attention to all family members, not just to the child with the chronic illness or handicap. Be as matter-of-fact and accepting of the children's descriptions as possible. As the children describe their families, highlight how their families are the same and different from one another. The concept of same and different is an important one that will emerge again during the workshop series. Thus, give these words a special emphasis as you speak.

Some children do not describe their brother or sister as having a particular handicapping condition or illness at this point in time, perhaps because they are not yet comfortable with the group or simply because they do not perceive it as relevant to what their family is doing in the picture. That is fine and it is common. Do not overinterpret the absence of mention of a child's disability or illness. Do not pressure the children in any way at this point to talk specifically about illnesses or disabilities. However, if other children begin to focus on their brother's or sister's problems, allow them to continue. Make sure that any words that they use that may be unfamiliar to other children in the group are defined. Once the children stop talking about their brothers or sisters and themselves, turn their attention back to their art work and other family members or activities within it. Praise the best features of their artistic attempts even if the overall quality of their production is lacking (e.g., *Boy, you pick out bright colors!*).

Because there is such wide variation in drawing skill and interest within this age group, some children will want to take 30 minutes or more with one picture, while others would rather draw many less detailed pictures. Once the children have completed their primary family pictures, allow them to draw a new picture of their own choice. You will keep their family drawings, while they will be allowed to keep their subsequent ones. The reason for keeping the family drawings is to be able to spend more focused time looking at them later. Often the task of managing the group and their discussion makes it difficult to see potentially important features of the children's drawings. End the family drawing activity by highlighting, again, the ways in which their families are the same and different from one another.

Bring the group to the star chart and put up a star for each one who completed a drawing before proceeding to snack. Give the children the option of helping you set up the snack or playing with each other in quiet, free play.

Activity 4: Snack (10–15 minutes)

Activity 5: Exploring Adaptive Equipment (5–10 minutes)

What you choose to show to the children will be determined, in part, by what is available to you. If you are conducting this group with children whose brothers and sisters do not need adaptive equipment of any kind, then this activity is optional. However, they may be exposed to the adaptive equipment in the classrooms or clinics that their brothers and sisters attend. This may be enough exposure to pique their interest and need for information.

Select for initial discussion pieces of adaptive equipment that we encounter almost daily. For example, eating utensils commonly used for infants and young children (e.g., bottle, cup with lid, small spoon with small bowl, booster seat) can demonstrate the principle of modifying tools to meet the characteristics and abilities of the intended user. In addition, this can show that at some point every-

one can need special assistance, even if they do not have a disability or illness and eventually grow out of their need.

Activity 6: Group Reading (10–15 minutes)

Select a book from your collection that is not obviously about a particular handicapping condition or illness but about illness or differences, in general.

Activity 7: Review, Reward, and Team Cheer (10 minutes)

Bring the children back to the easel where your star chart remains. Without emphasizing actual star totals for each child, show them with a broad sweep of your arm how many stars they received by knowing one another's names, asking good questions, drawing family pictures, and talking to one another. One-by-one give the children the first part of their participation reward (see Chapter 6 for more details on this).

Once the rewards are all delivered, reconvene the children briefly in a circle to lead them in the closing team cheer. This team ritual will be the last act of each group meeting and is intended to instill a special sense of camaraderie and fun as the children leave. To the best of your power, do not let a child leave with his or her parent before the final group cheer. Your final cheers could be as follows:

Remember the name we decided to call ourselves at the beginning of our meeting? Who can say it? (pause) Right! We are the "Sib Team." Well, not only do we cheer at the beginning of our meetings, but we will do it at the end of our meetings, too. Are you ready to do the cheer, "Two-four-six-eight," for the Sib Team? Okay, Team, huddle!

Huddle together, hand-in-hand in the middle of the circle. In a loud voice begin: *Two, four, six, eight! Who do we appreciate? The Sib Team! The Sib Team! Yeah!*

DISCUSSING CHILDREN'S DISABILITIES, ILLNESSES, AND STRENGTHS

GOALS

The primary goal of the second workshop is to promote discussion between the children about developmental disabilities and/or illnesses, in general. The key concepts of same and different—as they apply to objects and people—will be discussed during this session. The idea that two people or objects can be different from one another without one being better than the other will also be explored.

MATERIALS

The following is a list of materials to be used in this workshop:

Photographs
Star chart
Construction paper
Puppets
Adaptive equipment
Participation rewards
Heavy marker
Snack
Book for group reading

PREPARATION

You will need to become familiar with the photographs of flowers, cars, houses, and children that appear on the following pages of this workshop.

ACTIVITIES

There are 10 activities in this workshop. They are titled: greeting and team cheer; objects can be the same and different; people can be the same and different; relaxation exercise break; abilities can be the same and different; snack; adaptive equipment; group reading; review, rewards, and team cheer; and reminders.

Activity 1: Greeting and Team Cheer (5 minutes)

Activity 2: Objects Can Be the Same and Different (5–10 minutes)

Bring the children to the circle area, in front of an easel or around a table, and show them two of the photographs of different flowers (Figure 7.1a-d) (e.g., hibiscus, daisy, mum, lily). "Ask the group, *"Are these the same?"* Some kids will say "yes" and some will say "no." Then say, *"Jason, tell me, how are these the same?"* Elicit at least one similar feature from each child, such as, "Both are flowers," or, "Both need light and live in the ground." Then ask the children, about these same flowers, *"How are they different from one another?"* Again, have each child label at least one difference (e.g., different heights, shapes, sizes, smells).

Figure 7.1a-d.   Examples of different flowers.

Once the children grasp the concept of same and different as applied to the flowers, ask them, *"Which one is better?"* Expect a pause, since neither one is obviously better than the other. After the pause, restate your question as follows, *"Is one better than the other?"* If some children say "yes," ask them to explain. Usually, when this happens, the child says one flower is better because he or she likes the color or the smell more; it's a personal preference. If this happens, discuss how different people can like different things, but it doesn't make one better than another. Highlight how one person could pick the lily and another person pick the daisy and put them in their houses to admire equally. Emphasize again that two things can be the same in some ways, while different from one another in other ways and that one is not necessarily better or worse than the other. Repeat this line of questions with other flowers.

Next, present two photographs of different vehicles shown in Figure 7.2a-e (e.g., car, motorcycle, van). Repeat the discussion of same, different, better, and worse, as above. Follow this with discussion of different houses that appear in Figure 7.3a-e, which are also enlarged for display use.

Figure 7.2a-e. Examples of different vehicles.

Figure 7.3a-e. Examples of different houses.

110

Activity 3:   People Can Be the Same and Different (15–20 minutes)

Figure 7.4a-h depicts similarities and differences between children. Choose whichever photographs you feel might appeal most to your group of children before they arrive. However, at this point, you will not be using any photographs of children with visible handicaps or illnesses.

You will be displaying pairs of photographs of individual children whose appearances can be compared along numerous dimensions such as height, complexion, age, clothing, and gender. As you move through a series of questions similar to the ones you used in your comparison of objects, make sure you phrase the questions in such a way as to make it obvious that you are examining features of the children's external appearance. You will deal with the difference between appearance and behavior later.

Always remember to encourage communication between the children. One way to make this activity more fun is to encourage the group to repeat aloud the correct statements of the individuals. As they identify more and more features, they have to recite in chorus a longer and longer list of similarities and differences. Additionally, use the Freddy and Darla puppets to lead the discussion. You should expect your presentation to proceed something along these lines:

Darla: *Hi, everybody in the Sib Team! Remember me?* Encourage a loud affirmative response from the children in unison. *What? I couldn't hear you. DO YOU RE-MEMBER ME? My name is Darla, right?*

We saw before how things like flowers and houses can be the same as each other in some ways, while they are different in other ways, and that neither is better or worse than the other, right? Well, people—kids and grownups— can be the same and different in some ways, too.

Freddy: *Yeah, look at the pictures of those two kids on the easel. Who can tell me one way that they look the same?* Have Freddy call on one child, even if more than one shouted aloud. Have that child name a common feature of the two pictured children.

Darla: *Is that true? Do both children have the same color (hair)?* Encourage a chorus. *Okay, someone else now. How else do these kids look the same?*

Repeat these questions until each child has given at least one answer.

Freddy: *Okay, now, these children have the same _____,_____, and _____. But how do they look different?*

Repeat this question until each child has given at least one answer.

Darla: *Which kid is the better kid?* (Pause with a confused facial expression.)

Freddy: *Is either kid better than the other just cause they look different in some way? N-O!* Encourage a loud, group "NO!"

Repeat this sequence with two more different pairs of photographs. After the third pair, the children will probably need a break, especially if Activities 1 and 2 consumed 20 or

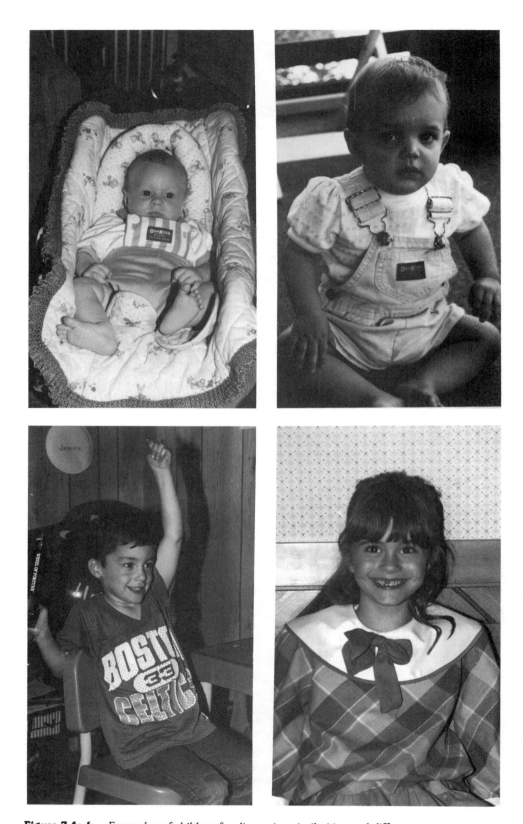

Figure 7.4a-h. Examples of children for discussing similarities and differences.

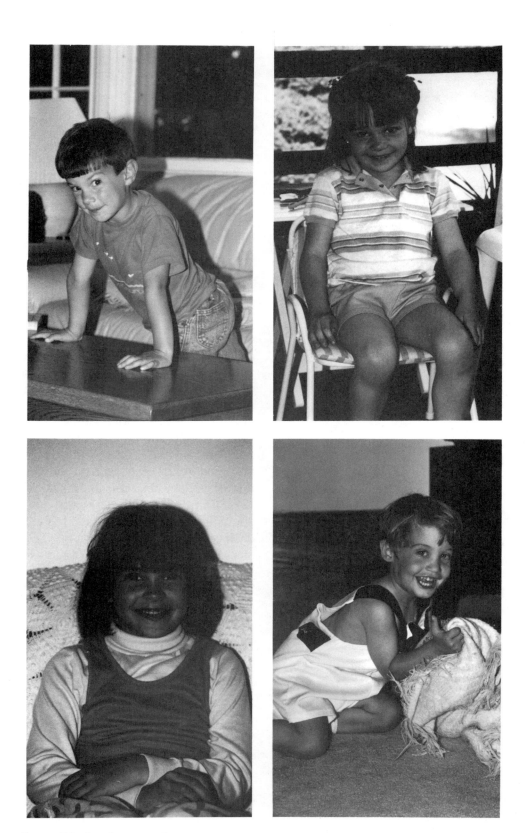

Figure 7.4a-h. *(continued)*

more minutes sitting around the easel. Put a star on their chart for co-operatively participating. For purposes of varying your presentation style, put Freddy and Darla away.

Activity 4:   Relaxation Exercise Break (15 minutes)

A helpful intervening activity that will not "overexcite" the children is to teach them modified progressive relaxation exercises. These are likely to keep them calm and quiet enough to be receptive to later group discussions. Progressive muscle relaxation exercises, in which the children tighten and relax groups of muscles, are relatively easy for young children to imitate and master.

For purposes of maintaining interest and variety, have the children sit in a circle on a carpeted floor, away from the easel. The Leader should sit in the middle of the circle. Have the children sit with their legs straight ahead (slightly bent at the knees, but not crossed) and their arms and hands resting in their laps. Provide a brief rationale to the children regarding the benefits of learning how to relax one's body. The words below are usually sufficient for introducing this activity:

Sometimes things happen that can make us feel upset or nervous. When this happens, the muscles in our bodies tend to get real tight and hard like this. Tighten the muscle of your arm and hold it while you continue talking and maybe turning red! *But when we are feeling good and are not upset, our muscles tend to be relaxed and calm.* Let your arm drop back into your lap. *I am going to teach you to pay atten-*

tion to the muscles of your body so that you can relax them and make yourself feel more comfortable at times when you might otherwise feel upset and tense.

Begin the exercises by holding out one arm, making a fist and tightening all its muscles. Hold that position for 5 seconds and comment aloud to the children about the sensations of tight, hard muscles (e.g., "My arm feels hard and uncomfortable. I can't do much with it so tight."). After 5 seconds, lower your arm to your lap and talk about your loose, relaxed, and tingling sensations. After this brief demonstration, have the children lie back, and lead them through a series of body parts, from the most mobile and visible (e.g., an arm or a leg, one at a time) to the more subtle (e.g., face, neck, stomach). With each alternating tensing and relaxing, verbalize and have them comment on the different sensations. This break should last about 15 minutes, after which you should return them as a group to their chairs at the easel. Put stars on their star charts for participating in the exercises. For more details on relaxation exercises for children, look at Berstein and Borkovec (1973).

Activity 5:   Abilities Can Be the Same and Different (20 minutes)

The concepts of same and different should be introduced at this time as they apply to children who have developmental or medical problems (see Figure 7.5a-i). Begin with a child representing a single sensory or motor impairment (e.g., the child wearing the eye patch or arm splint) and pair him or her with another who has

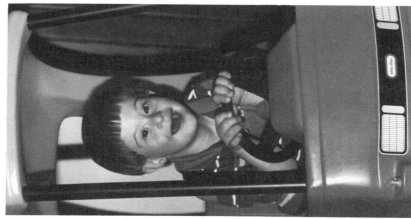

Figure 7.5a-i. Examples of children for discussing developmental or medical problems.

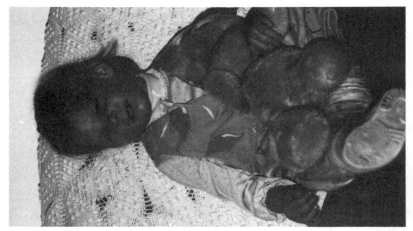

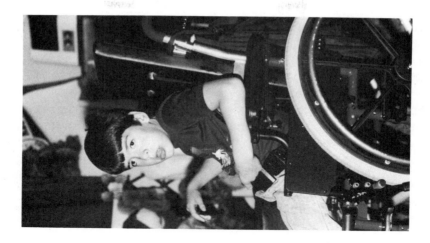

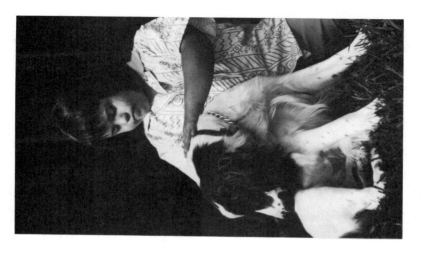

Figure 7.5a-i. *(continued)*

no visible signs of a difficulty. Remember that many of the problems that your group of children face are not visible. Thus, your use of the photographs should be modified to meet the interests of the children in your group. The following is an example of a typical verbal presentation using the photographs.

Now, here are two more children for us to look at. Jason, tell us one way in which these kids look the same. (Pause) Is he right, everybody? Do both kids have the same _____? Okay, how else do they look the same? Repeat until each child has identified one similarity. *Now, who can tell me something about how the children are different from one another?* Repeat until each child has identified at least one difference between the children's appearances.

Once a child mentions the depicted disability or adaptive equipment, this will become the first formal opportunity to have the children define what the disability is in their own words or for you to define it for them, should they have difficulty doing so. Remember that it is useful to hear what the children believe about various disabilities because their definitions and vocabulary should form the basis for your own definitions. Use the guidelines and glossary in Chapter 9 for examples of the wording and definitions of various conditions that children of this age appear to understand best.

Sometimes the children do not label the child's visible handicap or equipment as one of the ways in which the children look different from one another. If this happens, it should be identified and talked about with them. Set a tone that is desirable for use by the group in order to discuss various disabilities and illnesses. Through the example of a calm and matter-of-fact discussion of various illnesses or handicaps, any preexisting taboo about the topic may begin to diminish. You will be modeling for the children a way of talking about illnesses or handicaps that they will be able to draw upon in later conversation with their families, friends, and inquisitive strangers.

For example, if one of the children in the photograph is wearing a patch over her eye, your discussion could proceed as follows:

Yes, one child has a patch over her eye and the other child does not. Does anyone know what an eye patch can be used for? (pause) Sometimes people—kids and grownups—have one eye that has strong muscles and sees well, and one eye that has weaker muscles. Sometimes the weak eye doesn't always look where the strong eye looks. Since we want both eyes to be strong and work together, we do things to make the weak eye strong. We make it do muscle exercises. One way of making sure that the eye does its exercises is by putting a patch over the strong eye. This forces the weak eye to do all the looking and moving around. For an eye, looking and moving around are exercises. They make the eye strong. If the weak eye becomes as strong as the other eye, the patch can come off and both eyes can work together.

After such "diversions," return to your original line of questioning regarding same, different, better, and worse by saying, *Is one child better than the other?*

Based on their responses to this question that was asked earlier as well, the children are likely to say that neither child is better in general. Now is the time to help refine their thoughts about disabilities and illnesses. Introduce the idea that a disability may impair a child's functioning in one area of development without affecting another area.

> *Though one child isn't better than the other, he or she has some activities or skills that can be done well (e.g., singing) and others that he or she needs help with (e.g., seeing). The child sees well but needs help staying in the lines when coloring. So, just because someone has a kind of handicap or disability doesn't mean there aren't other activities that he or she can do well. We all have things that we are good at and not-so-good-at. Usually we cannot tell what somebody does well or not just by looking at them. You have to spend time together to get to know one another.*

Select about three more pairs of pictures, now including children whose disabilities or equipment are more apparent. Repeat the round of questions as before (*e.g., How do the children look the same? How do they look different? Is one child better or worse than the other?*). After the children have identified and discussed the children's disabilities, have them speculate as to the possible strengths that the children possess. Have each child identify at least one plausible strength for each of the pictured children.

If children recognize the adaptive equipment or features similar to their own brother or sister, it wouldn't be unusual for them to feel that he or she has a particular expertise in that area. Some children respond by explaining in detail the use and the foibles of the equipment. Such occurrences are desirable, as these children serve as models to the others that the topic of disability and illness are open for discussion. Quite frequently, the photographs of unfamiliar children with familiar abilities and disabilities lead the children into discussing their own family's situation. While a child should not be pressured to talk at this time about such matters, equal opportunity should be afforded to all of the participants.

At this point, the children will probably be restless. Their attention should be turned to their star chart. On the chart, put one star for each child who verbally participated in the previous discussion, and praise them for paying attention and helping the other children learn about each other. Offer them free time or the opportunity to assist in snack preparation.

Activity 6:   Snack (15 minutes)

Activity 7:   Adaptive Equipment (10 minutes)

If equipment that is similar to those discussed in the photograph sessions are accessible, consider having them available for inspection during this period. Always allow each child to handle the equipment and try to use it adaptively. Have more than one piece of each type of equipment available for the children.

Activity 8:   Group Reading (10 minutes)

Because the formal discussion of illnesses and disabilities has begun, books should be selected that portray particular conditions that may be of interest to the group. Encourage questions and expressions of personal experiences from the children.

Activity 9:   Review, Rewards, and Team Cheer (5 minutes)

Bring the children to where they will be able to see the star chart. Proudly tell them of the strengths in their behavior and cooperation during the meeting. Deliver the second piece of their participation reward and lead them in a team cheer before they leave.

Activity 10:   Reminders

If a good photograph of the children was not obtained during the home visit (see Chapter 6), remind parents to bring one to the next meeting. Additionally, ask the parents whose children use adapted devices to select an instrument to bring to the next meetings.

IDENTIFYING AND EXPRESSING POSITIVE EMOTIONS

GOALS

The goals of the third workshop are: 1) to improve the children's understanding of their own brother's or sister's disability or illness, 2) to encourage them to discuss it aloud with peers and to ask questions, 3) to increase their identification and verbal expression of the strengths of their brothers and sisters with and without handicaps, and 4) to increase the children's abilities to identify and verbally express their own positive emotions.

MATERIALS

The following is a list of materials to be used in this workshop:

Photographs
Star chart
Evaluation forms
Easel
Puppets
Snack
Construction paper
Miniature houses
Large hat or bowl
Book for group reading
Markers
Envelopes
Sibling personal photos
Participation reward
Human figure dolls
Adaptive equipment

PREPARATION

In order to lead the children in a discussion of the particular handicap-

ping conditions or illnesses of their brothers and sisters, you must become thoroughly familiar with the children's strengths and weaknesses. This will enable you to respond sensitively to each individual child within the group. As discussed in Chapter 6, spending time with each family in their home with all family members present is the best way to familiarize yourself with each group member's particular situation. However, it also is a goal to provide the children with general information and perspective on the handicapping conditions or illnesses of their brothers and sisters. Since no two children are alike, even if they carry the same diagnosis, you should learn about the range of possible symptoms associated with the diagnoses.

Because the easel will be in use during portions of your session, prepare a portable star chart for a clip board that can be carried between different areas of the room.

ACTIVITIES

There are eleven activities in this workshop. They are titled: greeting and team cheer; brothers and sisters can be the same and different; relaxation break; identifying and expressing positive feelings; snack; rehearsing praise with human dolls; brothers and sisters can be fun; adaptive equipment show-and-tell; group reading; review, reward, and team cheer; and mid-session evaluation.

**Activity 1:   Greeting
and Team Cheer (5 minutes)**

**Activity 2:   Brothers
and Sisters Can Be the
Same and Different (20 minutes)**

After greeting the children, gather them into a group around the easel. Put two of the photographs of children that were used at the end of the previous session on the easel in order to stimulate the children to recall the discussion of same and different. Use the following as an example of an introduction to the topics of the current workshop:

Remember last time we were together? We talked about how activities and people can be the same and different. We talked about how kids who have handicaps or who are sick are the same as other kids in some ways and different from other kids in some ways, too. We talked about these two children up here on the board, didn't we? Well, today we are going to talk about some more kids. Only this time we are going to talk about ones we know very well. Who wants to guess whom we are going to talk about? (Use your facial expression and voice to dramatize the intrigue of the situation.) *We are going to talk about you and your brothers and sisters today. We will find out how you all are the same and different, what your brothers and sisters are good at, and what they have trouble doing.*

How are we going to do that? Well, I have some pictures of you and your brothers and sisters here and I have some envelopes. (Give each child their respective photo-graphs and one envelope.) *Do these children look familiar to you? Do you know who they are? Well, say goodbye to them and put them into the envelope I just gave you. Tuck the flap in and put your envelope into this hat* (or whatever receptacle you are using). *Everyone is going to have a turn to reach inside the hat and pick one envelope. I will open the envelope and put the pictures up on the easel.*

Place the hat just above the children's eye level and lightly toss its contents. Encourage the first child to reach in and select an envelope. Dramatize the game to maintain the children's interest, by saying, *"I wonder whose pictures will be chosen!"* and, *"Now, who will be the lucky one?"* Once the child has made his or her selection, open the envelope and announce "the winner." Show the team the pictures, place a star on the photographed child's star chart (to assuage any embarrassment), and tack the pictures onto the easel. Have the child whose picture was chosen tell the group the name and age of his or her brother or sister.

Okay, team, now that we know the names of these two beautiful kids, let's see how they are the same and different from each other. Who can tell me one way that Heather and her brother look the same? Have the group decide on the "correctness" of each child's observation by asking the team questions such as *"Okay team, do they both have big eyes?"* Remember to encourage a unison response. Once each child, including the pictured child, has correctly identified one similarity, repeat the process but focus on how the children look different from one another. Once each child has identified a plausible difference, continue with your inquiry as in Workshop 2 as to whether or not one child is better or worse than the other.

It is often in this context of discussing differences that the child mentions that his or her brother or sister has a handicap or illness and he or she does not. If this topic is raised in this manner, pursue a full discussion of that particular condition. If the topic does not come up, however, you should raise it as soon as the group has completed its discussion of other obvious differences. While more attention may be focused on the child within the group whose pictures are on the easel, carefully ensure that you also address the group as a whole. If more than one child has a brother or sister with the same diagnosis, do not require a second definition of that condition. Remember to encourage the children to talk freely and to ask and answer questions of each other. The glossary within Chapter 9 provides examples of definitions of common handicaps and illnesses that are suitable for young children. In addition to assuring that a fairly accurate definition of the condition is learned by the group members, each child will also be encouraged to describe plausible strengths of each depicted child. Your discussion of each photographed pair may proceed along the following lines:

Okay, Chad and his sister Mary are the same in some ways and different in others. Chad said that Mary has cerebral palsy and he doesn't. That is one way in which they are different. Chad, please tell the rest of the team what you know about cerebral palsy. (Allow time for his response.) Can anybody else tell us some more? Well, what we know is that the words "cerebral palsy" are used when kids and grown ups have had trouble moving parts of their bodies ever since they were babies. The brain inside of our heads helps to send messages to our arms, legs, and tongue—to all parts of our bodies really—and tells them how to move. The brain tells your body when to start moving and when to stop moving. Sometimes when babies are born, something can happen that can make it hard for their brains to get the right message to the rest of the body. Some people who have cerebral palsy have only a little bit of trouble moving just one part of their body while other people have trouble moving almost every part of their body. Sometimes people use other big words like "diplegia" and "hemiparesis" when they talk about cerebral palsy. Chad, does your sister seem to have trouble moving parts of her body? Tell us the kinds of activities that she can have trouble with.

If another child's sibling has the same diagnosis, encourage that child to dominate the discussion with Chad so that the individual variability can be highlighted.

Now I want you to tell us some of the things that your sister can do well, parts of her body that she doesn't seem to have trouble with. Since it is sometimes hard to think of good things to say about our brothers and sisters, I'll put an extra star next to your name on the star chart for each good thing that you can tell us about your sister. But you can't make up things that aren't true just to get an extra star. You have to tell us at least two good things that your sister can do or fun activities that the two of you sometimes do together.

(If the child being discussed has severe multiple handicaps, you will be able to help the children focus on the less apparent but important abilities such as holding her head up, smiling, and rocking to music.) Verbally praise each sibling for portraying their brother's or sister's skills in a reasonably accurate way. To end each discussion about particular sibling pairs, encourage some other child in the group to briefly summarize what he or she has learned about the handicapping condition or illness that was just discussed (e.g., Well, Chad and his sister helped us talk and learn about cerebral palsy. Who can tell me what they learned before we pull another envelope with pictures out of the hat?). As soon as one other child comes up with an accurate definition, praise that child for listening and telling the group what he or she has learned and place a star next to his or her name on the star chart. Place a star next to the name of the child who was discussed and return to the next child in line to select a new pair of "mystery" photographs.

Ideally you should be able to get through all sibling pairs within 20 to 30 minutes, but if your group is large, talkative, or bored, break up the activity with relaxation exercises. Maintain possession of the children's photographs since they will be used again in a future workshop.

Activity 3: Relaxation Break (10 minutes)

Bring the children to the carpeted floor and repeat the progressive muscle relaxation exercises conducted during the second workshop. Solicit volunteers from the group to assist you as a relaxation leader.

Activity 4: Identifying and Expressing Positive Feelings (10–15 minutes)

The purpose of identifying and expressing positive feelings is to assist the children in learning how to identify positive emotions in themselves and others and to practice expressing them verbally.

Return the children to their chairs near the easel. Perch Freddy and Darla upon your knee and have them greet the team as if they are their long lost friends. Manipulate both puppets to have sad looking faces and then ask the children if Freddy and Darla look like they have heard good news or bad news—do they look happy or sad? Then manipulate more cheerful expressions—mouths open and upturned, arms upraised. Because you want the children to focus first on nonverbal facial expressions of happiness, do not accompany your expressions with any vocal cues such as giggles or laughs. Then ask the children again if Freddy and Darla feel happy or sad? Most children do not have any problems discriminating between happy and sad facial expressions on the puppets.

Have the children select one puppet of their own from the collection. One-by-one, have each child demonstrate how his or her puppet looks when it feels happy. Encourage the children to be quiet, and to manipulate only their puppets' faces. As each child creates a positive face with his or her puppet, have the other children decide if the expression truly is happy or sad. Instruct the children to affirm a correct positive expression with a positive expression of their own (using the puppet) and to respond to any negative expression with a sad or disappointed expression of their own.

Once the children are reliably creating positive and negative facial expressions, it will be time to explore the other ways in which positive, pleasant emotions can be expressed. Have Freddy or Darla tell the children to cover their eyes with their puppets so that they cannot see Freddy's face. Have Freddy laugh aloud with a silly, comical laugh. Have the children manipulate their puppets' faces to indicate what Freddy was probably feeling when he made that sound. Though most children will identify the exaggerated laugh the first time they hear it, they usually find it funny enough to warrant repeating. Point out that another way to know how people feel is to listen to their voices. Allow each child a turn to use his or her voice to express something positive or negative while the others cover their eyes with their puppets. As before, have the team indicate the emotion through facial expression with their puppets, but this time allow them to respond with a similar voice. Have the children put their puppets aside for a minute so that the ideas

above can be practiced with their own faces and voices.

Once the children appear fluent in identifying emotions, it is time to practice identifying interpersonal situations that frequently result in positive emotions. The simple acts of verbally praising and complimenting will be demonstrated first through the use of Freddy and Darla. (The children should not be wearing their puppets at this time.)

Freddy: *Boy, you are all good at figuring out when people feel happy by looking at them and listening to them. Now we're going to figure out some of the reasons why people feel good. Darla is going to help me out on this one first. Right, Darla?*

Darla: *Right! Now, team, I bet that you know that if you say certain kinds of things to people you can give them good feelings. That's what I'm going to do to Freddy— say something that is going to make him feel good. But first I have to figure out something good. I know! I'll tell him that he looks nice today. Freddy, you look very nice today.*

Freddy (with a big smile in response): *Thank you. You look especially nice today too.*

Darla (to Freddy with a smile): *Thank you.*

Darla (to the group): *How did Freddy feel when I told him he looked nice? And then what did Freddy do? Yes, that's right. He felt good and ended up saying something to me that made me feel good too. Let's try that again. Who can help me out here and whisper something in my ear that I can tell Freddy to make him feel good?* Put your ear to each child and act on the first compliment or praise statement you hear, repeating this game until each child figures out something pleasant to say, either to Freddy or to Darla. Immediately have the puppet receiving the praise respond with something equally pleasant.

See what happens when you find something nice to say about people? They often find something nice to say or do in return and everybody ends up feeling pretty good. One of the ways all of you make me feel good is by doing all of these activities together and playing nicely with each other. Maybe if I tell you how great you're all making me feel and maybe if I put another big star next to every one of your names on this star chart, you will feel pretty good, too. How is that? Doesn't it feel good when the whole team gets stars? It also feels good to eat snacks, right? Well let's get ready for them now.

Activity 5:   Snack (10 minutes)

Activity 6:   Rehearsing Praise with Human Figure Dolls (15–20 minutes)

Use this activity or Activity 7 to elicit role-playing and discussion of positive situations with brothers and sisters. If time allows, do both activities; however if you must do one or the other, use the human figure dolls with children who enjoy creative doll play.

For those who need more structure, use Activity 7, which is based on discussion of the photographs found on pages 128–131.

Bring the children to the group table. Help the children build a town with your collection of miniature houses, shrubs, and dolls. Allow each child to select the house that he or she wants to "live in" and the human figures that are to be the family members. The children will be using the dolls to create expressions of praise and positive emotions within their families. Encourage them to be as realistic as possible in the scenes that they create. You will be giving them a star on their chart for every positive statement they create. However, rather than determining yourself whether each child has created positive scenes, have the other children decide and instruct you as to whether or not a star should be entered next to the child's name.

Once the children have constructed the imaginary town and selected their family members, your play sequence might go something like this:

Now that you have all built this cozy town and have your families ready, each one of you is going to show us with the dolls some of the nice things that the people in your family do. Practice doing or saying some nice things in return, also, just like we did with Freddy and Darla before. For each nice thing that you say for each person in your family, the rest of the team will decide if it really is nice or not. If you really do say or do something nice, the rest of the team will tell me to put a star next to your name on your star chart. You have to make sure that what you do or say is something that that person in your family really can do; don't make up crazy stories with your dolls. Who wants to get an extra star for going first?

Okay, that's great, Betsy. You will be first. Let's start with your mother. Show us your mother doll. What is something good or nice that your mother does with you or for you? (Remember to have the rest of the team judge the "goodness" of the statement.) *That is something that makes you feel good when your mother does it, right? Pretend that she is doing that now and show us what you could do or say to her that would make her feel good, too. That's great, now let's do the same with your brother. What is something that he is good at or something that he does that makes you feel good?* (Repeat this for each family member and for each child.)

Activity 7: Brothers and Sisters Can Be Fun (15 minutes)

The photographs prepared for this activity depict some of the positive aspects of young sibling interactions. Bring the children together around the group table, place a photograph on the table, and tell an imaginary story about the child who is pictured. Then ask a series of follow-up questions to encourage the children to acknowledge the positive aspects of their relationships with their brothers and sisters. These stories should evoke conversations of feelings of pride, companionship, closeness, affection, nurturance, teaching, and appreciation. If, for some reason, the siblings in your group do not label those feelings, encourage them to do so, by commenting, *"Maybe Ashley feels proud of herself for being a good leader and feels proud of her brother for learning to swing the bat so well."*

Story 1 *This girl is Jacqueline (see Figure 7.6). She is 6 years old. She has two little brothers, John and Peter. John is 3 years old and Peter is a little baby. He is about a year old. Jacqueline has a bottle of bubbles for blowing big bubbles. Her brothers are too little to blow bubbles so Jaqueline blows bubbles for them.*

Figure 7.6. Jacqueline and her two brothers, John and Peter.

How does Jacqueline feel when she blows bubbles for her brothers? Why?

How do her brothers, Peter and John, feel? Why?

What would her mother or father do or say if they saw Jacqueline?

Story 2 *The boy is Jeremy (see Figure 7.7). He's 4½ years old and* *he has a twin sister whose name is Linda. Linda has Down syndrome, but Jeremy does not. Jeremy has a special computer game that he can only play with another child, so when he wants to play his computer game with someone, he asks his sister to play.*

Figure 7.8. Sarah and her brother Henry.

Figure 7.7. Jeremy and his twin sister Linda.

How does Jeremy feel when Linda plays the game with him? Why?
How does Linda feel when Jeremy asks her to play? Why?
How do Jeremy's mother and father feel when he and Linda play the computer game together? Why?

Story 3   *This is Sarah (see Figure 7.8) who is 5 years old and her brother Henry who's 3. Even though Henry has trouble walking, he doesn't have any trouble swinging in the swing. Sarah's and Henry's father takes them to the park and pushes them on the swings right next to each other.*

How does Sarah feel when her father takes her to the park with Henry? Why?
How does Henry feel being on the swing beside Sarah? Why?

How does the father feel pushing both kids together? Why?

Story 4   *Here is Matthew (see Figure 7.9) who is 3 years old. He has a new baby brother named Lee. At first, Matthew wasn't sure about having a baby in the house. He didn't really know about babies. They got a lot of company with everyone who wanted to see the baby. But instead of looking at the company, baby Lee just wanted to look at his big brother, Matt. Sometimes when his mother is right there, Matt holds the baby in his own lap.*

How does Matthew feel when the baby looks just at him? Why?
How does the baby feel about Matthew? Why?
How does Matthew's mother feel about Matthew and the baby looking at each other's faces?
How does the mother feel about Matthew holding the baby carefully when she is there? Why?

(Note: Make sure you emphasize to the group that they cannot hold

Figure 7.9.   Matthew and his brother Lee.

babies unless adults are around to help.)

Story 5   *Amy is 7 years old (see Figure 7.10) and her sister Laurie is 3. When their parents go out at night, Amy and Laurie stay together with a babysitter. Sometimes they are allowed to stay up later together, so they play with Laurie's peg boards and other toys.*

Figure 7.10.   Amy and her sister Laurie.

How does Amy feel about being home with Laurie when they have a babysitter? Why?

How does Laurie feel with Amy around? Why?

Story 6   *Ashley is almost 8 years old (see Figure 7.11) and her brother, Tom, is 4. Tom wants to learn how to play baseball, so Ashley shows him how to swing the bat. Tom learns how to swing and actually hits the ball.*

Figure 7.11.   Ashley and her brother Tom.

How does Ashley feel about teaching Tom something fun? Why?
How does Tom feel about learning from Ashley? Why?
How do their parents feel?

Story 7   *Hillary is 7 years old (see Figure 7.12) and her sister, Cindy, is 10. Her sister has trouble learning in school. Hillary and Cindy do their homework at the same time. Sometimes Hillary helps Cindy do her homework, even though Hillary is younger.*

Figure 7.12. Hillary and her sister Cindy.

How does Hillary feel about helping her older sister with her homework? Why?

How does Cindy feel about Hillary helping her?

How do their parents feel about them working on their homework together?

Story 8 *These boys are 6½-year-old Emmet and his older brother Cliff (see Figure 7.13). Cliff has a wheelchair because he cannot walk. He has cerebral palsy. Emmet knows when Cliff wants to go into the bathroom and volunteers to push his chair for him.*

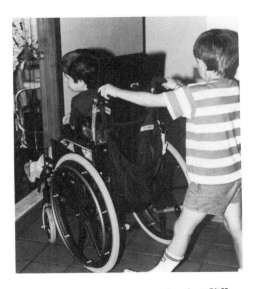

Figure 7.13. Emmet and his brother Cliff.

How does Emmet feel about helping to push the chair? Why?

How does Cliff feel about getting help from Emmet? Why?

How do their mother and father feel about them both? Why?

Story 9 *These three girls are sisters (see Figure 7.14). The oldest sister, Liana, won this great big polar bear at an amusement park. She is letting her other sisters, Tina and Maria, have a ride on it.*

Figure 7.14. Liana and her sisters Tina and Maria.

Why does Liana let her sisters have a ride?

How do her sisters, Tina and Maria, feel about being on the polar bear? Why?

How does Liana feel? Why?

What do you think their mother and father are gonna feel and say?

Activity 8: Adaptive Equipment Show-and-Tell (10 minutes)

As had been encouraged the previous week, some of the children should have with them a small piece of their brother's or sister's adaptive or therapy equipment. Allow each child to demonstrate and describe what they have brought to show-and-tell. Praise each child for being informative and thorough in his or her presentation and for asking appropriate questions about the equipment.

Activity 9:   Group Reading (5–10 minutes)

Activity 10:   Review, Reward, and Team Cheer (5 minutes)

Focus the children's attention on their star chart and with a sweeping motion, again praise them for the large quantity of stars that they have earned by participating in the group activities. Briefly mention the activities completed during the session. Deliver the third part of their participation reward and lead them in their team cheer.

Activity 11: Mid-Session Evaluation

Give parents the evaluation questionnaires to complete on their own and with their child. (See Chapter 8's Program Evaluation for evaluation forms.)

IDENTIFYING AND EXPRESSING NEGATIVE EMOTIONS

GOALS

The goals of the fourth workshop are to increase the children's abilities to identify and constructively express negative emotions. More than any other session of this series, Workshop 4 focuses the children's attention on the potential stressors of having a brother or sister who is chronically ill or handicapped. The children are encouraged to freely discuss with one another some of the sadder feelings and experiences that they may have encountered or are likely to encounter due to their brother's or sister's problems. The goal is to provide peer support along with the special feeling that none of them is totally alone in their experience. The long range goal of this workshop is to introduce the children to alternative means of coping with some of their more upsetting situations. The workshop, however, is not to be an unstructured gripe session, as young children of this age need assistance to identify and articulate sources of their emotional discomfort. Without constructive discussion and guidance, you run the risk of simply agitating them without apparent benefit. Their conversation should be structured as in previous workshops, with the prepared content serving as a likely beginning point for sharing personal experiences.

While you will be providing the children with the opportunity to express and discuss some of the more frustrating or negative aspects of their situations, you will also be teaching them some creative problem-solving skills. By encouraging the children to generate and rehearse numerous solutions to the same problem, you will introduce them to the fact that there is often more than one way to approach a problem and that solutions become obvious only once you have shared your concerns with others.

MATERIALS

The following is a list of materials to be used in this workshop:

Illustrations
Star chart
Puppets
Book for group reading
Participation reward
Snack

PREPARATION

The illustrations on the following pages have been especially prepared for this important workshop. Prior to the group meeting, review all illustrations and the stories that accompany them. The order of your presentation of the stories should be graded from the least to the most complex and potentially distressing so that the children can accustom themselves to the process. Experience with this workshop series suggests that the example stories appropriately depict the children's concerns without overwhelming them. However, if the accompanying illustrations and stories do not capture a situation that you consider to be important for your group to discuss, consider modifying the stories to better meet your group's specific needs. You may consider using one of the other photographs from an earlier workshop to meet these individual needs.

If your experience with the group leads you to expect that a certain child or family may have particular difficulty identifying and expressing negative emotions, consider the possibility of spending a little extra time with that child's parents to review this workshop's activities. Help prepare them for the possibility that their child may come home primed to talk about some of the more difficult aspects of their family life. If the parents are attuned in advance and have the opportunity to briefly prepare themselves with you and each other, they may have a more satisfying interaction and conversation with their child.

ACTIVITIES

There are six activities in this workshop. They include: greeting and team cheer; brothers and sisters aren't always angels (Parts I and II); relaxation exercises; snack; group reading; and review, reward, and team cheer.

Activity 1:   Greeting and Team Cheer (5 minutes)

Activity 2:   Brothers and Sisters Aren't Always Angels—Part I (30 minutes)

Have the children sit in chairs in a semicircle or around the group table. It is important that they be able to position themselves to see the pictures easily. The children will often huddle intensely over one another in order to see the pictures, which generally does not result in any problems. In fact, when the children assume such a position, they seem to work better as a team.

Below is a recommended style and content of introduction of these activities, along with the stories accompanying each illustration. Again, Freddy and Darla can be helpful in maintaining the children's attention to your introductory comments.

Freddy (with an angry face): *Darla, I'm not feeling very well today. I don't think that I want to talk to these kids very much.*

Darla: *Why not? What's the matter?*

Freddy (to Darla): *I feel like going into my room. My brother is driving me nuts and I don't know what to do.*

Darla (whispering to the group): *Did you know that he has a brother? I didn't! (to Freddy): Well that's too bad that you are feeling this way. What happened?*

Freddy: *He ate the last ice pop and now there's none left for me. He always gets everything and I get nothing. I wish I had a sister instead of a brother. My friend Johnny has a sister and I don't ever see her do mean stuff like take the last ice pop. I wish I lived in a family where everybody was happy and nice to each other all the time.*

Darla (to Freddy): *WHOA! WHOA! Did I just hear you say that you want to live in a family where everybody is happy all the time, like every minute of every day?*

Freddy: *Yeah! That's what I said.*

I want to live in a perfect family like my friend Johnny. Then I would be happy.

Darla: *Wait a minute, Freddy. There's no such thing as a family where everybody is that happy all the time. That would not be normal. People just aren't like that, so families just aren't like that either.* (to the children): *Right, team? Is there a family on earth where everybody is happy for every minute of every day, where everything is always perfect, and where nobody ever gets in any trouble? Is there a family where even the babies are born with smiles on their faces and never cry when they are hungry? Come on, team, tell Freddy that "Real families are not perfect."* (Give the children time to tell him and then make them shout it louder, in unison.)

Freddy: *You mean even if I had a different brother or sister I might not be able to get my own way and be happy all the time with them either?*

Darla: *That's right!* (to the children): *Does everybody here have fights or arguments or get mad at their brothers and sisters every once in a while? Aren't everybody's brothers and sisters a pain once in a while?*

The majority of children will admit that their brothers and sisters can be annoying. Take note of any child in the group who does not dare admit to everyday sibling frustrations. Do not confront the child and make him or her admit that their brother or sister can be a pain, but do attend to how they respond to the rest of the workshop. A child's reluctance to share

even minor annoyances may be a sign that it is not part of the family style to regularly express negative feelings verbally. This may be a child whose family you choose to spend extra time with at the end of the session.

Darla (to Freddy): *Well, Freddy, I think that the kids have given you something to think about. Maybe you and I can leave them for awhile and let them talk about it some more. Would you like that?*

Freddy (to Darla): *Yeah. It kind of makes me feel better to know that other families and other kids have trouble with their brothers and sisters sometimes.* (to kids): *Well, thanks everybody. I think I'm going go take a walk and think for a little while. See you later. Come on, Darla.*

Adopting the conversational tone and direction of the group leader again, it is time for you to get the children ready to talk about other sibling stresses.

It looks to me like Freddy had reason to be upset with his brother. Everybody can get upset, right? But Freddy just did not know what to do with himself and wanted to go to his room and sulk because his family isn't perfect. I'm glad that you were all able to tell him the truth about how families are in real life. Sometimes people do things that annoy or hurt the other people in the house and it's not because they don't love them.

Today we are going to look at pictures and I am going to tell you some stories about children who find themselves in situations that they don't like. Since you all make such a good team, you are going to listen to the stories together, figure out what is bothering the children, and think up ways that could make them feel better. You are all going to come up with good ways to help the children out. Let's start with the first picture and story and see how we do.

After you tell each story you will ask a question that encourages the children to identify the feelings of the people depicted in the illustration. You will then ask a series of questions designed to get them to think about things that could be said or done to help them feel better or to cope with the situations. After each child provides a response to the question, encourage the other children to verbally repeat that solution as a team, in unison (e.g., *"Okay, let's try Henry's answer."*). Once at least three alternative solutions are offered by the group, have the children practice each suggestion in unison and in succession (e.g., *"Yes, he or she could cry or could find something else to do or could tell someone that he or she feels sad."*). Strongly emphasize the word "or" so as to highlight that each problem has many viable solutions to consider. Do not be surprised if a child proposes a rather violent solution to a problem situation (e.g., "I'd punch him in the nose if he did that."). Simply ask some follow-up questions that will cause the children to judge the possible outcomes of their own solutions (e.g., "Well, he could punch the boy in the nose, but then what would happen?"). Usually other children in the group will help the child decide that he or she should not include aggressive suggestions as one

of the alternatives. However, if the children do not want to abandon it as a possible alternative, you can lead them to rephrase and soften the statement to some degree (e.g., *"I'd want to punch him in the nose."*) To not recognize this as an alternative may communicate an air of censorship to the children when your primary goal is to get them to brainstorm and evaluate the many possible solutions.

Often an illustration becomes the departure point for more personal discussion. Though the children themselves are not depicted, they may recognize the dilemma portrayed and want to tell of a specific experience that they have had personally. If this happens, guide the discussion toward how the particular child felt in the situation and how he or she reacted and coped. Suggestions from the other children regarding these very real confrontations should be most welcomed and rehearsed in much the same manner as their responses to the illustrated vignettes. Having such a discussion occur as a result of the stories and illustrations is a major goal of the workshop, not a digression. Patiently allow the child to share his or her experience and allow the discussion to evolve. Return to the structured story format when it becomes clear that the children have run out of avenues to discuss on their own.

Story 1 *You see this child standing in the doorway? (see Figure 7.15) Well, he is around 6 years old and he has a brother who is 2 years old. This brother is very healthy. This boy (the one at the doorway) just came home from his friend's house and wants to go into his* *room to play his tape recorder. But look what he finds when he gets there. His little brother was playing in the room when he shouldn't have been there and made a big mess. His little brother even ruined his favorite tape. If his mother or father sees the room, they will be angry at the older boy because he is supposed to keep his room neat.*

Figure 7.15. Identifying and expressing negative emotions.

How does the big brother feel? Why?

How does the little brother feel? Why?

What can the older boy say to his little brother?

What should he say to his parents?

Story 2 *This little girl is four (see Figure 7.16). She has an older sister who is having a birthday party. Her older sister is wearing a new dress and is opening presents.*

While her older sister is in the other room, the little girl sees the delicious birthday cake and wants a piece of it. She asks her mother if she can have a piece, but mother says that she cannot because it is for her sister's party.

Figure 7.16. Identifying and expressing negative emotions.

How does the little girl feel? Why?

How does she feel about her older sister?

How does she feel about what her mother says?

What can the girl say?

Story 3 *This girl, Julia, is 6 years old (see Figure 7.17), and she has an older sister who has to go to many doctors. It seems like she is going to a different doctor or teacher every day. Julia always goes to the doctors' appointments with her mother and sister. Julia waits in the room with them while the doctor talks to her mother. They use big words and she doesn't know what they are saying.*

How does Julia feel? Why?

How does the sister feel? Why?

How does the mother feel? Why?

What can the little girl say?

What can the little girl do?

Figure 7.17. Identifying and expressing negative emotions.

Remember to give the children feedback on their cooperativeness and talkativeness during the discussion by using their star charts.

Story 4 *This boy is 5 years old and he has a little sister who has a handicap (see Figure 7.18). The sister has trouble moving her legs and needs special exercises. A physical therapist comes out to the house every week and shows his mother new exercises to do with his sister. Sometimes the physical*

Figure 7.18. Identifying and expressing negative emotions.

therapist brings toys and special equipment that look like a lot of fun, but the boy is not allowed to use it because it's special and only for his sister.

How does the little boy feel? Why?
How does the sister feel? Why?
How does the mother feel? Why?
What can the little boy say to feel better?
What can the little boy do to feel better?
What might the mother and therapist do so that everyone feels better?

Activity 3: Relaxation Exercises (10–15 minutes)

It is likely that the children will become somewhat fidgety, if not from the topic, then from having to sit for so long. It is recommended that an intermission take place at this point in which one or two of the children lead the group in their relaxation exercises. One of the benefits of having the children do relaxation during their break rather than having a free play time, is that you can remind them that they can use their relaxation responses to cope with some of the difficult or distressing situations that have been discussed.

Remember to put stars on the children's charts for participating in the relaxation sessions.

Activity 4: Brothers and Sisters Aren't Always Angels—Part II (15–20 minutes)

Continue with the illustrations and stories as in the first part. Allow a little time for the children to become interested again.

Story 5   *Here is another child named Amanda (see Figure 7.19). On her way home from school, a new kid whom she wants to be friends with asked her if she could come over. Amanda tells her that she will ask her mother and then call her back and let her know. When she gets home, Amanda's mother says that she cannot bring a friend over that day because her brother had a seizure* (explain what a seizure is if necessary) *and is very tired and sleeping.*

He has a 6-year-old sister who needs to be fed and really cannot move much at all. His sister still needs help in the bathroom and then taking a bath. Jonathan also has a 2-year-old brother. His brother doesn't really have any special problems but needs a lot of help because he is only 2 years old. Because mother is busy with his sister who is handicapped, father asks Jonathan to make a peanut butter and jelly sandwich for his 2-year-old brother.

Figure 7.19.   Identifying and expressing negative emotions.

Figure 7.20.   Identifying and expressing negative emotions.

How does Jonathan feel? Why?
How does his father feel? Why?
What can Jonathan say?
What can Jonathan do?

Story 7   *This boy's name is Ray (see Figure 7.21). Ray was planning to go to the beach with his family, but his little sister got sick again so Ray is now going to stay at home with his grandmother while his parents take his sister to the hospital.*

How does Ray feel? Why?
How do Ray's parents feel? Why?

How does Amanda feel? Why?
How does the mother feel? Why?
How does her new friend feel? Why?
What can Amanda do to feel better?
What can she say to her mother and her new friend?

Story 6   *This is Jonathan (see Figure 7.20). He is 4¹/₂ years old.*

Figure 7.21. Identifying and expressing negative emotions.

What can Ray say to feel better?
What can Ray do to feel better?

Story 8 *This family is going to the zoo (see Figure 7.22). Brad is almost 7 years old and is helping his parents by pushing his older brother in his wheelchair. His older brother has a handicap and is littler than Brad even though he is older. Sometimes Brad's brother does weird things with his hands. While Brad is on line for the zoo, he notices that a couple of children on line are pointing at his brother. He thinks that he heard one of them call his brother a "retard."*

How does Brad feel? Why?
How does his brother feel? Why?
What can Brad say?
What can Brad do?

Figure 7.22. Identifying and expressing negative emotions.

After you have gone through each of the illustrations, give the children positive verbal feedback for discussing some of the difficult situations that were portrayed in each picture.

Activity 5:   Snack (10 minutes)

Activity 6:   Group Reading (5–10 minutes)

Activity 7:   Review, Reward, and Team Cheer (5 minutes)

Remind the children of the day's activities and praise them for talking to one another about some of the difficult aspects of having a brother or sister who has special needs. Point out the number of stars on the group chart. Deliver the fourth piece of their participation reward and end with an exuberant team cheer.

HIGHLIGHTING SIBLINGS' STRENGTHS AND TALENTS

GOALS

The goal of the fifth workshop is to focus the children's attention on their personal strengths and talents. The workshop is designed to enable them to testify verbally about their own personal strengths. After the fourth workshop, which focused on stressful experiences, and after paying much attention to all other family members throughout the workshop series, individual attention to the sibling is warranted.

MATERIALS

The following is a list of materials to be used in this workshop:

Illustrations
Star chart
Poster board
Markers
Participation reward
Sibling personal photographs
Paints
Safety scissors
Tape or glue
Book for group reading

PREPARATION

Prior to the group meeting, tape or tack one large piece of poster board for each child along a wall at child height. The children will be constructing posters that testify to their kindness, strengths, and abilities. Have their personal photograph available since they should become part of their posters.

On the following pages, a group of simple line drawings can be found with positive self-statements on them (see Figures 7.23–7.29). Either trace or photocopy the drawings provided in this volume or draw similar ones of your own. Have enough copies of each drawing available for every child.

ACTIVITIES

There are seven activities in this workshop. They include: team greeting and cheer; selecting compliments for other group members; snack; group reading; adaptive equipment or relaxation exercises; positive self-posters; and review, reward, and team cheer.

Activity 1: Greeting and Team Cheer (5 minutes)

Activity 2: Selecting Compliments for Other Group Members (20–30 minutes)

Point out the poster board that is hanging along the walls of the room and tell the children that they are going to make big posters that show their greatness. Next, have the children sit around the group activity table where paper and art supplies are available. Instruct the children to

I   AM   NICE

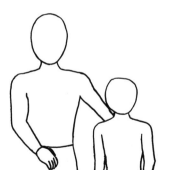

Figure 7.23.

I   AM   FUN   TO   BE
AROUND

Figure 7.24.

I   AM   SMART

Figure 7.25.

I   AM   STRONG

Figure 7.26.

I   AM   HAPPY

Figure 7.27.

I SAY NICE THINGS

Figure 7.28.

I SHARE

Figure 7.29.

begin working on two drawings for their poster: a self-portrait of them doing their absolutely favorite activity, and an outline of their hands on the paper. Encourage them to help the child next to them draw their hands.

Once the children are settled and busy, take each child aside in a quiet and private corner of the room where the other children may be able to observe but not hear any conversation. Take out the simple line illustrations that have positive self-statements written on each drawing (you will want to make copies in advance so these are readily available). Explain to the child that he or she should pick out the saying and drawing that he or she would like to give to each of the other children in the group. Encourage the child to select the drawing that best suits each of the other children. Most children need quite a bit of structure and encouragement for this aspect of the activity, so do not be overly concerned if you dominate the child's choice. Once this child has selected a drawing for each of his or her peers, write the child's name on each picture, as well as for whom the picture is intended. Instruct the child to return

to the group table to finish his or her self-portrait and hand silhouette, and to begin coloring or painting the drawings that he or she has selected for his or her peers. To promote intrigue and interest, instruct the child to not tell anyone else what the two of you did together since it will be a surprise. Once that child is settled at the table and drawing, call another child to join you in the corner. Feel free to assign additional time-filling drawing or coloring activities to any child who nears completion of the original assignments before his or her turn for the corner arrives. Once each child has made his or her selection, allow the group ample time to complete their coloring. Because the children may not all finish at the same time, allow them to look at the reading and picture books on disabilities or illnesses and to assist you in the preparation of an early snack. Put a star on their star charts for each picture they complete with care.

Activity 3:   Snack (10 minutes)

Activity 4:   Group Reading (10–15 minutes)

**Activity 5:   Adaptive Equipment
or Relaxation Exercises (10 minutes)**

**Activity 6:   Positive
Self-Posters (20–30 minutes)**

After the adaptive equipment session
or relaxation exercises, bring the children to the wall where the poster
boards have been hung. Assist them
in writing their first names at the top
of the board that they choose for
themselves. Give each child their photograph to glue atop the poster. Once
completed, have them glue their recently completed self-portraits any-
where onto the board.

The next step is to hand out the
drawings that each child selected for
the others. Arrange the pictures face
down in random order and have each
child take a turn randomly selecting
from the array, as in a card game.
Have the child hand the selected paper to you so that you can announce
whom the picture is for, who it is
from, and what it says. Be dramatic
and entertaining with each revelation
of who is giving what picture to
whom. Have the child-recipient step
forward to his or her poster to glue the
picture onto it, but only after saying
aloud, and with confidence, the positive self-statement that appears on
the drawing. Make sure that the child
verbalizes the statement in an audible

voice. Lead the rest of the team in a
unison repetition of what the child
says. Repeat this for each drawing
and child so that by the end, each
child has produced many positive
self-statements and has heard many
nice comments announced about
him- or herself by his or her peers.

The final steps in constructing the
posters will be to have the children
spontaneously generate their own
positive self-statements, independent
of the statements that appear on the
drawings. For each positive statement that is generated, draw a colorful illustration on the poster, and encourage the children to decorate their
posters in any other way that they
please. The children are usually very
proud to take their posters home at
the end of the workshop.

**Activity 7:   Review, Reward,
and Team Cheer (5 minutes)**

Review this session by reminding the
children of how very special they are.
Compliment each child on his or her
poster, and praise the group for earn-
ing stars on their star charts. As you
deliver the fifth part of their participation reward, remind them that next
week is their last formal meeting and
that they will be able to take their participation reward home then. Finally
lead them in the team cheer.

1 2 3
4 5 6
7 8 9
10 11 12

EVALUATING THE
CHILDREN'S EXPERIENCES

GOALS

The goal of the final workshop is to review all of the concepts that have been discussed during the previous sessions and to have the children and their parents evaluate their experiences. By now, the children should be well aware that this is the last formal meeting of the team as part of the workshop series. Though you may feel sad that the series is coming to a close, it is important that the children leave on the upbeat. The children should end their session with a strong feeling of accomplishment, a sense of having learned something about disabilities and illnesses, and a gladness for having made connections with other children who can easily understand their unique situations. Most of all, they should leave thinking that they have had fun.

MATERIALS

The following is a list of materials to be used in this workshop:

Photographs, illustrations
Star chart, Bingo boards
Evaluation forms
Hat or bowl
Participation rewards
Small prizes
Adaptive equipment

PREPARATION

In order to review the greatest number of concepts with the least amount of boredom and repetition, a board game based on the game "Bingo" can be played. You may duplicate the game board that is shown in Figure 7.30. Have one game board for each child in your group. The numbers on the game board have been arbitrarily assigned to represent the various goals and objectives of the workshop series. If you have added any unique goals or objectives to your workshop series that do not appear in the pages that follow, make sure that the Bingo game is modified accordingly.

Print the letters and numbers of the modified Bingo board onto small pieces of paper that the children will be able to select from a hat. These will also serve as their playing pieces, so make them of sturdier construction paper or cardboard. Make one playing piece for each box on each child's Bingo board. Have one small prize ready for each child. These can be single cans or plastic bags of homemade Play doh, coloring books, stickers, markers, or any other small trinket that can serve as a prize for completing the Bingo game.

After the structured curriculum activity, you should plan a special party with snacks that are better than the usual fare. Additionally, if you can arrange transportation with parents, it is great to end the structured workshop

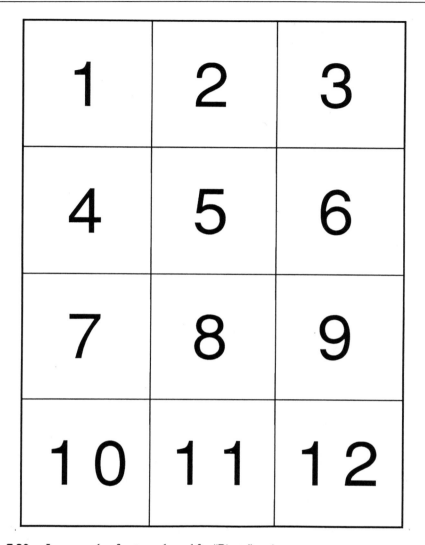

1	2	3
4	5	6
7	8	9
10	11	12

Figure 7.30. An example of a game board for "Bingo" review.

after only one hour, followed by a group trip to a local attraction (e.g., zoo, park). Parents can be invited.

ACTIVITIES

There are five activities in this workshop. They include: greeting and team cheer, Bingo review, snack, de-

livery of final participation reward and evaluative feedback, and special outing and team cheer.

Activity 1: Greeting and Team Cheer (5 minutes)

Have the children rally around the carpeted floor in a circle. The day's activities can be introduced in a manner similar to this:

Today is a pretty special day for this team, isn't it? Who knows what today is? (Remember to encourage them to answer.) Well, today is special because it is our last meeting together as a weekly group. Since it is our last weekly meeting, we will do some special things. We will play a game that is like Bingo to go over all of our team work and things that we have learned and talked about here. And after that, we are going to finish up our special participation rewards, have a party, and go to (the zoo). Since we are going to have such a busy day, I think we should get started. Are you ready to cheer? Let's go!

Activity 2:　Bingo Review (30 minutes)

Bring the children to the group table where the Bingo boards and a hat or bowl with numbered slips of paper have been placed. Explain the following game rules to the children.

During all these weeks we have been talking about so many different things—about how children are the same and different, what different disabilities and illnesses are, how we can figure out and tell people our feelings, and so on. Today, we will go over some of our team work again to make sure that everybody remembers it when they leave. Like I said before, we will play our own special Bingo game. One by one, each of you will take a turn picking a little card out of this hat (or bowl). Each card has a number on it that matches one of the numbers on your Bingo board. When you show me the number I will ask you to tell me something or to do something that is similar to one of the things that we did during our workshop meetings. Maybe the number you pick will make you have to say two nice things about yourself or your brother or sister, or maybe the number you pick will say that you have to tell me what the word (deaf) means, or maybe you will have to look at some pictures of children and make a good guess as to how they are feeling. After you give your answer, the rest of the team will decide if you get the question right or not. (When the rest of the children decide, remember to dramatize their answers through unison and repetition.) If the rest of the team decides that your answer is right, you will be able to put the little card on the same number on your board and then the next person will take a turn. If the team decides that your answer is not really right, then you will give your card to the person sitting next to you and he or she will have a chance to answer the question. If nobody can answer the question, then I answer it and the little card goes back into the hat! Whoever fills up their board with cards first, gets to pick a prize from the collection. There are enough prizes for each one of you to get one when you cover every number on your board with a card. Okay. Is everybody ready?

Assuming that you will have approximately six to eight children in your group, below are suggestions for questions that can be asked and assigned to arbitrarily numbered curriculum objectives. Modifications of these questions will need to be made in order to cover any personalized goals of the sessions. Make sure to include questions that pertain to the particular disabilities or illnesses that you discussed that may not have been explicitly discussed in this workshop guide. The questions below should be used as a guide to the level of complexity that should be addressed at this time:

1.   Disability or Illness Questions When a child selects the disability or illness questions card, the following examples can serve as possible questions:

What does the word handicapped/ mental retardation/cystic fibrosis mean? (Insert pertinent terms for your group.)

How come some people use their hands to talk to other people?

Can children catch Down syndrome from their brothers and sisters?

Can someone who has juvenile rheumatoid arthritis learn to ride a bicycle?

What kind of handicap or illness does your brother or sister have?

Name two people or places you could go if you wanted to learn more about your brother's or sister's handicap or illness.

2.   Adaptive Equipment If a child selects the number for adaptive equipment, allow him or her to demonstrate and explain to the group the use of any of the available pieces of adaptive equipment. Also, consider some of the following questions if you do not have enough pieces of equipment to go around:

Give me one reason why a child might use an eye patch.

Tell me two different ways that people can make their wheelchairs move.

How can someone who is blind read a book?

If a big person has trouble tying his or her sneakers but does not want his or her parent's help getting dressed, what kind of sneakers might he or she get?

If someone wants to learn how to drive a car but cannot use his or her legs to push the gas pedal or brake pedal, what could be done to the car so that that person can learn to drive?

What are two ways that someone might be able to communicate or talk to other people even if they could not speak or make sounds?

3.   People Can Be the Same and Different When a child selects the card about people being the same and different, put any two photographs from Workshop 2 on the easel. Ask the child the following three questions for each photograph pair:

Tell me one way that these two children look the same.

Tell me one way that these children look different from each other.

Is one child better or worse than the other?

4.   Progressive Relaxation If the child selects the progressive relaxation card, have him or her demonstrate to the group the successive tensing and relaxing of one body part after answering the following question:

When would be a good time to use your relaxation exercises at home?

5.   Identifying Positive Emotions and Family Characteristics If the

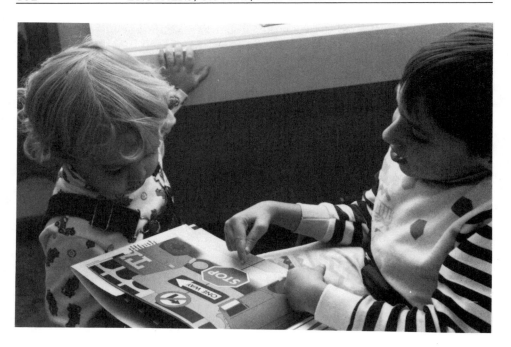

child selects the number for identifying positive emotions and family characteristics, he or she should answer one of the following questions:

Tell me two nice things about your mother.

Tell me two things that your father did especially for you or with you during the last couple of weeks.

What are two activities that your brother or sister can do well without any help at all.

Tell us two things that you do with your brother or sister that almost nobody else can get him or her to do.

Name three things that your friends in this group think you are good at.

6.   Identifying and Coping with Stressful Situations   If the card for identifying and coping with stressful situations was picked, the child should answer one of the following questions:

How would you feel if you could not go to your friend's house because your brother or sister needed to go to the doctor? What might you do or say if that happened?

How would you describe your brother's or sister's handicap or illness to a new friend who was coming to your house for the very first time?

How would you feel if other children were teasing you and your brother or sister? What might you do or say to them?

What would you do or say if your sister or brother with a handicap got really mad at you and hit you?

How would you feel if you could ride your bike without training wheels but your older brother or sister had to stay in his or her wheelchair?

Rotate through these similar questions until one child has succeeded in covering his or her Bingo board with tokens. When that child gets "Bingo," allow him or her to select one prize from the array of small prizes. Remind the remaining players that they, too, will collect a prize after completely covering their Bingo board with tokens. Even after some children have collected their prizes, have them remain within the circle of activity until all have finished the game.

Activity 3:   Snack (10 minutes)

Activity 4:   Delivery of Final Participation Reward and Evaluative Feedback

In order to give the children the last remaining pieces of their participation rewards, take each one aside and make it a special time. Make each child feel how special he or she has been to you and tell them some unique thing that they did during the workshop series that you will always remember. Before letting that child leave your side to go back to the general room, assign the child a small activity or task to keep him or her busy and out of trouble, such as completing their workshop evaluation chart, so that you can have a moment of relatively uninterrupted time with the next child (see Chapter 8 for sample evaluation forms).

Activity 5:   Special Outing (Optional) and Team Cheer

Before departure, have the children huddle as a group. Tell them all how great they were as a team and have them yell one last team cheer together.

SUMMARY

The workshop activities described in this chapter have been designed for children ages 3½–8 years whose brothers and sisters have a variety of medical and developmental problems. The activities are designed to provide information and peer support to young siblings as they face their unique pleasures and challenges with their families.

CHAPTER 8

PROGRAM EVALUATION

THERE ARE THREE MAJOR ASPECTS OF PROGRAM EVALUATION that should be considered in regard to the sibling workshop series. First is an evaluation of consumer satisfaction. Second is the evaluation of changes in sibling knowledge, attitude, or behavior as a function of participating in the group. Related to the latter is whether or not the siblings meet the workshop goals of improving understanding. The third aspect of program evaluation to be considered is the workshop series' effects on the siblings' behavior at home. While it isn't possible to evaluate the long-term effect of the workshop program on sibling development and family relationships, the techniques that are described can be sensitive to the more short-term effects of the program. Your choice of evaluation techniques will probably be determined by your goals and resources.

CONSUMER SATISFACTION DATA

Parents, as well as siblings, are the consumers of the workshop series; therefore, opinions of both groups should be canvassed in order to make the program most responsive to the needs of the entire family. While it is best to encourage ongoing contact with parents by speaking to them briefly at the close of every meeting, a formal evaluation questionnaire can encourage more thoughtful and considered feedback. Some individuals feel they can be more honest and unbiased when completing a form than when faced with the person who is requesting the feedback.

Parent Satisfaction Survey

It is recommended that a standard evaluation questionnaire be sent home half way through the workshop series as well as at the end of the series. Including a mid-series questionnaire provides parents with the opportunity to contribute information that may affect their own child's participation in the activities. If you wait only until the end of the series to obtain formal parent input, then their information cannot be used to benefit their own child, only future participants who may differ substantially in their needs.

Figure 8.1 presents a sample questionnaire that can be modified for use during the middle and at the end of the workshop series. Permission is granted to copy the Parent Evaluation Questionnaire on pp. 158–159, or you can make your own. Pass this on to parents at the end of the third workshop along with a stamped, self-addressed envelope. Request that they return it within a few days and before the fourth meeting so that you will have enough time to review the feedback and make any adjustments. The questionnaire that the parents complete at the end of the series should be returned within one week of the end of the series or returned during a follow-up home visit if such an evaluation is conducted.

Sibling Satisfaction Data

Obtaining valid and useful feedback from young children who participate in the sibling workshop is a challenge. Due to their immaturity of judgment, they will be best able to tell you how much they liked or disliked an activity—not necessarily its growth promoting potential. They are very limited in their ability to evaluate how much they learned from a particular activity or group experience. Often, there is little or no agreement between what young children report they like and what is good for them. However, knowing whether or not the children enjoy the activities is important. If the children are routinely bored or overly upset by a particular activity, then they will be less likely to pay attention and gain anything from the activity. Also, boredom or unchecked discomfort are more likely to result in disruptive behavior. Conversely, if the children enjoy the activities, they will be more inclined to absorb the information and talk about the group experiences with family and friends. Such conversations, as you know, can offer their own long-term benefits within the family.

When obtaining feedback from siblings, it is wise to keep two ideas in mind: the opinions that they express about an activity are quite vulnerable to their feelings at the time the opinion is requested, and what they report to their sibling group leader may differ from what they report to their parents. These two tendencies have concrete implications for action. First, obtain the children's opinions about a specific activity as soon as the activity is through. Do not wait until the end of the session, after a string of different activities. If you do wait, the feedback that the children provide about the activity will be contaminated by their feelings toward whatever else occurred between the time of the activity and their evaluation of it. Figure 8.2 presents a type of sibling activity feedback chart that the children can use to provide feedback at the end of each activity. This, too, can be copied from p. 161, or you can make your own. Use a fresh chart, with a new activity number written for each activity, so that the children are not influenced or distracted by their previous notes. If you use this chart regularly, the children should become proficient

PARENT EVALUATION QUESTIONNAIRE

Please take some time to answer each of the questions below about your child's participation in the Sibling Workshop Series. Be as honest and open in your answers as possible. Thank you for your time and attention.

Date: _____ Name of workshop leader: _____

Group meeting time and location: _____

_____

_____

Rate your satisfaction with the following aspects of the groups on a scale from 1 (very dissatisfied) to 5 (very satisfied).

		Very dissatisfied				Very satisfied
1.	Group meeting time	1	2	3	4	5
2.	Group meeting location	1	2	3	4	5
3.	Length of each meeting	1	2	3	4	5
4.	Group composition	1	2	3	4	5
5.	Communication and contact with workshop leader	1	2	3	4	5
6.	Workshop format	1	2	3	4	5
7.	Workshop activities/content	1	2	3	4	5
8.	Opportunities for parent input	1	2	3	4	5
9.	Impact on your child's knowledge of disabilities or illnesses	1	2	3	4	5
10.	Impact on your child's feelings toward his or her brother or sister	1	2	3	4	5
11.	Impact on your child's feelings toward other family members	1	2	3	4	5
12.	Impact on your child's self-image	1	2	3	4	5
13.	Quality of the workshop series, overall	1	2	3	4	5

14. Has your child talked about what has happened during the meetings?   Yes   No
    Comments: _____

_____

_____

15. Has your child seemed to enjoy the group meetings?   Yes   No
    Comments: _____

_____

_____

16. Was there any particular activity that your child seemed to have really enjoyed?
    Yes   No
    Comments: _____
    _____
    _____
    _____

17. Has your child seemed upset by any meeting?   Yes   No
    Comments: _____
    _____
    _____
    _____

18. Has any particular activity made a strong impression on your child?   Yes   No
    Comments: _____
    _____
    _____
    _____

19. What do you think your child has learned from the workshops? How has he or she benefit-
    ted so far?
    Comments: _____
    _____
    _____
    _____

20. Is there any way in which you feel your child may have been harmed by the workshop
    activities?   Yes   No
    Comments: _____
    _____
    _____
    _____

21. Overall, are you glad that your child participated in the workshop series?   Yes   No
    Comments: _____
    _____
    _____
    _____

22. Is there anything we should consider for future workshops to make them more enjoyable
    or infomative?   Yes   No
    Comments: _____
    _____
    _____
    _____
    _____

23. Any other comments: _____
    _____
    _____
    _____
    _____
    _____
    _____
    _____

Thank you for your time and feedback!

Figure 8.1.   Sample Parent Evaluation questionnaire that can be used at mid-session or at the end of the workshop for parent feedback.

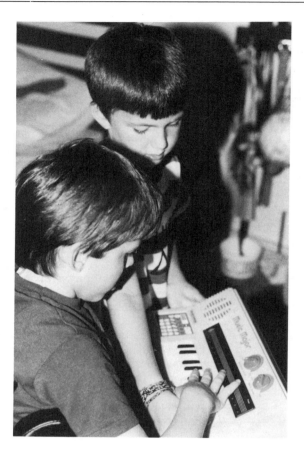

at providing quick feedback and the exercise will not be disruptive to the group process. All children should be given their own feedback sheets to mark independently and they should be discouraged from looking at one another's papers. You might consider explaining the feedback form like this:

> It is very important to me to know whether or not you like the activities that we do together, so every once in awhile I will ask you to let me know what you think by using this piece of paper. If you liked or had fun during the activity, then you can draw a circle around the smiling face. If you didn't like the activity at all or if you felt bad because of it, you would put a circle around the angry or sad face. If you thought what we did was just okay—not great, but not bad either—then you'd put a circle around the straight, regular face. Just circle the one that shows me how you liked what we did. You don't have to look at anybody else's circles, just your own.

One other way to obtain information from the children is to send home a questionnaire to be completed jointly by the children and parents. This may prompt a discussion between them about

Sibling Activity Feedback Chart

Read immediately after each activity: Circle the face that shows how the activity we just did made you feel. If you really liked what we just did, circle the face with the smile. If you thought that it was "Just OK," not great, but not bad either, then circle the face with the straight mouth. If you really did not like what we did, then put a circle around the frowning face.

Activity Number	GREAT	JUST OK	BAD

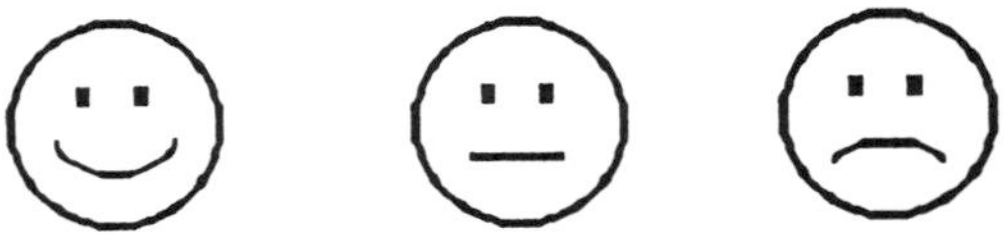

____

Figure 8.2. Sample of a Sibling Activity Feedback chart to be used at the end of each activity.

the group, an attractive side-effect of this procedure. Figure 8.3 depicts a sample questionnaire that would be given to parents midway through and at the end of the series when parent satisfaction survey forms are distributed. (Permission is granted to copy the Sibling Workshop Evaluation Questionnaire on pp. 162–163.) When giving the sibling satisfaction/evaluation form to parents, explain that it is useful, but not essential. If the child does not want to talk about the group experience with the parent, assure the parent that it would not be the first time a perfectly healthy child adopted that attitude. Encourage the parent to wait a few hours, even days, before trying the activity again. Always encourage the parent to listen openly to the opinions and feelings that are expressed by the sibling about the experience, even if that opinion differs from their own. Encourage parents to find some individual time to spend with their child to complete the questionnaire in order to minimize distractions. This individual time can be rewarding and satisfying to the child.

ACQUISITION OF SIBLING WORKSHOP OBJECTIVES

This session details two ways in which sibling acquisition of the workshop objectives can be evaluated. They are through a group review and individual sibling role play assessment.

Group Review

The modified version of "Bingo" that was played by the siblings in the last workshop of the series provides an opportunity to review the children's attitudes and behaviors that are relative to the specific

SIBLING WORKSHOP EVALUATION QUESTIONNAIRE

Note to Parents: Try to spend some time alone with your child to discuss his or her participation in the Sibling Workshop Series. If your child resists the conversation or working with you to complete this form, do not push it further, but wait a few hours or days to try again. Read each question to your child, then encourage his or her response. Please listen to your child's opinions openly and write them down as accurately as possible, even if these opinions differ from your own. If you and your child end up having an important conversation and cannot finish the form in one sitting, try to arrange another time to complete it. Thank you for your time and commitment.

Date: _____   Name of workshop leader: _____
Group meeting time and location: _____
_____
_____

1. Do you like going to the brothers and sisters group?   Yes   No
    Why? _____
    _____
    _____

2. What do you like the most about the group? _____
    _____
    _____

3. What don't you like about the group? _____
    _____
    _____

4. I am going to name some of the activities that you do in the meetings. Tell me if you like them, don't like them, or think they're "just OK." If you don't remember which activity I'm talking about, tell me that you don't.

	Like	Dislike	Neutral	Don't remember
a. Team cheer (e.g., 2-4-6-8!)				
b. Freddy and Darla puppet shows				
c. Reading books on problems				
d. Talking to other brothers and sisters				
e. Relaxation exercises				
f. Drawing and talking about our families				
g. Getting stars				
h. Snacks				
i. Talking about "same and different"				
j. Looking at pictures and telling stories				
k. "Bingo" review				
l. Making big posters about yourself				

5. Do you think other children whose brothers and sisters have a problem would like to go to a group like this too? _____

_____
_____
_____

6. Are you glad that you are going to the brothers and sisters group?   Yes   No
Why? _____

_____
_____
_____

7. If there's another workshop when you're older, do you want to go to it,
too?   Yes   No
Why? _____

_____
_____
_____

8. Is there anything else that you want to tell me about the brothers and sisters
group?   Yes   No
Why? _____

_____
_____
_____

Thank you for your time and feedback!

Figure 8.3. Sample Sibling Workshop Evaluation Questionnaire to be given to the parents to complete with siblings at mid-session and at the end of the workshop.

workshop objectives. This can reflect the children's knowledge about the discussed topics upon leaving the workshop series, but provides no indication of changes due to their workshop enrollment since the game was not played before the workshop series began. The advantages of using this Bingo game technique are that it can be played with the children as a group and is already incorporated into the workshop series. Furthermore, the children generally enjoy the activity and associated rewards.

Sibling Role Play Assessment

One way to evaluate change in the siblings' attitudes or understanding that could be attributed to the group would be a before-and-after comparison or a pre-post test. While there are many standard child behavior checklists and questionnaires available on attributes such as self-esteem, these probably would not be sensitive to immediate workshop effects (Lobato, 1985). In order to tap specified changes relevant to the workshop series, the Sibling Role Play Assessment technique was developed (Lobato, 1981, 1985).

Children of preschool or kindergarten age often respond more freely to questions asked in a play context than to those asked directly in an interview format. The role play technique described below can be useful to obtain information from young siblings regarding their ideas on disabilities and diseases, in general, as well as the specific problems of their brothers and sisters. The game also offers the opportunity for the siblings to describe themselves and other family members.

The Sibling Role Play Assessment requires approximately 20 minutes to complete and can only be conducted on an individual basis, one child at a time. It should be completed, first, during the preliminary home meeting, and then, within the week after the last workshop. The evaluation session should be audio recorded (with parent permission, of course) for later study and analysis. Reviewing and analyzing the 20 minute tape along the lines that are suggested later will require at least another hour. The time required to conduct the assessment and to analyze the children's responses may make it prohibitive for some users. An abridged version can be considered wherein just questions tapping the sibling's ideas on disabilities and diseases are presented.

Guidelines for the administration and interpretation of this type of assessment appear below.

Administration Guidelines   The Sibling Role Play Assessment consists of a series of scripts involving the use of small human figure dolls and other objects to set up simulated interactions between the sibling and other adults and children. Make the interactions as realistic as possible by changing the pitch and inflection of your voice for each character that you assume, by dramatizing all appropriate actions involved with the dolls, and by using relevant toy props (e.g., couch, bed) for the settings of your interactions. Decide what important disability or illness terms you will ask the child

to define before you begin. Since you may have an idea of the problems of other potential workshop participants, you may include some of those terms. Limit your questioning to no more than five disability or illness terms.

You can be playful and spontaneous as you set up each scene, but once it is set up, you should use the wording presented in the scripts to prompt the children's responses. After children respond, do not give them feedback (e.g., the response is: good/bad, right/wrong). Try to remain as neutral to the children's responses as possible. Encourage them to elaborate on their responses by using minimal prompts such as repeating what they have just said but in question format, saying "uh-huh," "go on," or by upturning a questioning eye-brow in their direction.

Script Codes   The scripts contain the following codes down the left hand column.

VSU (Verbal Set-Up)   VSU's are the comments that you should make to set the scene up for the child. Try to match the wording or phrasing closely, but there is room for some spontaneity in order to get the particular child interested and involved. You should use your regular adult voice when speaking.

OI (Other Instructions)   OI are instructions to you that should not be spoken to the child. They should help you move smoothly from one action to the next.

VP (Verbal Prompts)   VP are the comments that you should make to the child to elicit their particular thoughts on important topics. These should be spoken word-for-word as they are presented in the script. If a particular child does not respond, then you may try paraphrasing, using as close an approximation to the standard prompt as possible. These verbal prompts should be spoken using the type of voice of the "person" you are pretending to be.

Role Play Scripts   The following are role play scripts used to elicit comments regarding family members, self-reference, and disabilities and illnesses.

Eliciting Comments Regarding Family Members

VSU   *Okay, now we're going to play a game where you can set up a house and choose people to be your family. I have all these great pieces of furniture and people in my bag that we will use. Would you help me set up the house? We'll make believe it's your house, OK?*

OI   Take the furniture out of the bag room-by-room, keeping all other props and dolls hidden so that the children can be surprised. Start with the kitchen, then the living room set, then the child's bedroom, then nursery (if applicable). Let the child have enough time to enjoy setting up, but move him or her along with encouragement and promises of the toys yet to come (e.g., "I have more furniture when you've finished with this room.") Once the child has set up the house, say:

VSU   *What a nice job you did setting up the house. Now it's time to get your family so they can be in your house. I have dolls in here that we can make believe are your family, friends, and neighbors.*

VP   *We'll start with your family. Tell me, who is in your family?* (child responds, if no response, then . . .)
      What are the names of the people in your family? (if no re-sponse, then . . .)
      Okay, there's you, there's your mother, there's. . . .

VSU   *Who should we put in the house first?*

OI   If child says him- or herself, encourage a different family member by saying:

VSU   *Let's make believe you are outside playing so you won't be home first. Pick somebody else.*

VP   Okay (family member's name). *What can you tell me about* (name) *before I look for him? Tell me about* (name).

OI   Make believe you are looking for (name).

VP   *What does* (name) *do at home?*

VP   *Is he (or she) happy or sad? Why?*

VP   *Is there anything else you can tell me?*

VSU   *Okay, I think I have found* (name) *in my bag. Here he (or she) is. Put him (or her) in the house's living room to wait for the next person. Okay, now, who else do we need?*

OI   Repeat the above sequence of verbal prompts about a sec-ond family member. Continue the sequence until all family members except the child him/herself are described.

Eliciting Self-Reference Comments

VSU   *Okay now, almost everybody in your family is home, but you are still outside playing with a friend. While you're outside, a new neighbor comes over to meet your family. I'll be the new neighbor. You be your mother.*

OI   Have the adult neighbor doll knock on the imaginary door and encourage the child to answer the door through the mother doll.

VSU   *Hi. I'm your new neighbor. I wanted to come over to intro-duce myself and to meet you.*

OI   Have dolls shake hands.

VSU   *Gee, is this your family?*

VP   *I thought you had another child, a girl (or boy) about _____ years old? Do you?*

OI   Here you will elicit the child's statements about him- or her-self as they speak to the neighbor through the mother doll.

VP   *I have a child the same age, maybe they can be friends. Tell me about* (child's own name) *and I'll tell my boy (or girl) about him (or her) when I get home.*

OI   When the child finishes, make believe that it's time for the neighbor to go back home.

VSU   *Well, I have to go home now. It was nice meeting you all. I hope I'll see you again soon.*

OI   Have the neighbor doll go back in the bag.

Eliciting Comments about Disabilities and Illnesses

VSU   *I think it's time now to make believe that you and your friend come home. Let's find a doll that can be you and one that is your friend.*

OI   Take two child dolls out of the bag and have the child pick the ones he or she wants to use. Have the child tell you his or her friend's name.

VSU   *Okay, now I'll make believe that I'm* (friend's name) *and you make believe this is you.*

VSU   *That was fun playing outside together. Let's go to your room to play and talk some more.*

OI   Have friend doll lead child doll to a separate bedroom. (They can skip and hold hands along the way.)

VP   *Before we start playing games, I need to ask you some questions because I think you might know the answers. Last night when I was with my mother, she said that a new family moved into the neighborhood, that we have new neighbors. She also said that the new neighbors have a little boy/girl* (sex of child's own sib) *who has* (disability or illness). *I never heard that word before. Could you tell me what it means to have* (disability or illness)?

OI   Remember that you should decide the diagnosis that you want the child to describe prior to the start of the session. Insert your terms where the words appear in parentheses below.

VP   *Anything else you can tell me about* (disability or illness)?

VP   *Are children with* (disability or illness) *happy or sad? Why?*

VP   *What can children with* (disability or illness) *do?*

VP   *Is there anything else you can tell me so I can understand better?*

VP   *What if this child had* (disability or illness), *what would that mean?*

VP   *Anything else you can tell me?*

VP   *What can children with* (disability or illness) *do?*

VP   *Are children with* (disability or illness) *happy or sad? Why?*

VP *My mother also said the word* (disability or illness). *What does that mean?*

VP *Does* (disability or illness) *mean anything else?*

VP *Are children who have* (disability or illness) *happy or sad? Why?*

VP *What can children with* (disability or illness) *do?*

VP *My mother also used the word* (disability or illness). *I've never heard that word before. What does it mean?*

VP *Anything else you can tell me about the word* (disability or illness)?

VP *Are children with* (disability or illness) *happy or sad? Why?*

VP *What can they do?*

VP *One last question, and then let's play with your toys. What does* (name child's sibling's diagnosis) *mean?*

VP *Anything else you can tell me about* (sibling's diagnosis)?

VP *What can children with* (sibling's diagnosis) *do?*

VP *Well, thank you for answering my questions. Those were all words I never heard before. Now what do you want to do together?*

OI Allow the child to set up a play scene and assume whatever role the child wants you to play. Continue for a few minutes with this scene and then end the session gently by putting the toys away and turning the child's attention to something new.

Interpretation Guidelines The Sibling Role Play Assessment has been used to evaluate previous uses of the Sibling Workshop Series (Lobato, 1981, 1985). The questions regarding sibling's definitions of various disabilities and illnesses are fairly straightforward and have good face validity; however, because the technique has not undergone in-depth evaluation, the children's verbalizations about themselves and family members should not be over-interpreted. This information will be most useful when used in conjunction with other observations and information. Previous research has shown, however, that there is good correspondence between the way young children describe their siblings and the way their relationship is characterized by their mothers (Dunn, 1985).

A tape recorder should be used during the assessment to capture the child's verbalizations because the person actually conducting the assessment will be so busy and involved with the child. The child's verbalizations on the tape can then be carefully analyzed at a later time for his or her knowledge of relevant diagnoses and for statements regarding self, siblings, and parents.

Knowledge of Relevant Diagnoses First, the accuracy of the child's knowledge of various illnesses or disabilities can be assessed. Listen to what the child says in response to the questions that ask for a definition of a particular diagnosis. Children's definitions can be categorized as accurate, partially accurate, or completely inaccurate. We do not expect young children to use sophisticated language, but they can often produce definitions similar to those presented in Chapter 9. Accurate definitions are those in which the child mentions the core aspect of the illness or disability. The child does not have to describe the cause or details of the diagnosis to be considered accurate. Some real examples of accurate definitions are: "Kids who are retarded just learn slower," or "Cystic Fibrosis and CF are the same thing. It means you have trouble breathing and need to take special medicine." Partially accurate definitions include those in which the child shows a mixture of understanding and misunderstanding. For example, when a 4-year-old said, "Blind means somebody poked you in the eye with a stick," he demonstrated an appreciation that blindness had something to do with the eyes, but revealed a lack of understanding of cause. A similar partial understanding of diabetes is reflected in this comment by a 5-year-old boy: "Diabetes is when you eat too much sugar and it gets stuck in your teeth and blood. It also can give you cavities." Children's inaccurate definitions are quite easy to recognize. They range from the frank statements of, "I don't know" to often amusing inventions. Examples of completely inaccurate definitions include statements such as, "Deaf means you can't see" or, "When I turn 7 years old, I might get cerebral palsy too."

As the children define various handicapping or illness conditions, they often reveal other ideas and misconceptions about their brother's or sister's situation. Opportunities to correct these misconceptions should be arranged during the workshop series. However, if those misconceptions remain at the time of the post test when you are administering the Sibling Role Play Assessment after the series has ended, the child should be corrected right there. Also discuss the child's ideas with his or her parents following the assessment, and suggest ways for the parents to follow through on that issue.

Statements Regarding Self, Siblings, and Parents   A comparison of the children's statements can also be made about themselves, their sibling with a chronic illness or disability, and other family members. Statements and descriptions that the children make about themselves can be categorized as positive, negative, or general/neutral in emotional tone. If, during the assessment, a child describes him- or herself as "the smartest child in the family," this would be considered a positive self-reference statement. A negative self-referent would be any comment in which the child insults or refers to a negative aspect of his or her own appearance, behavior, or personality. Also included would be comments in which the child states that others feel negatively toward him or her. For example, consider the following negative self-referents: "I can't do anything right" or, "My father calls me stupid." General self-reference statements are those comments in which the child describes a personal characteristic in neutral or nonjudgmental terms. Examples include: "I have blue eyes" and, "I share a room with my sister." Once you have categorized the child's self-referents in this way, calculate ratios of the number of positive, negative, and general statements that have been made above the number of all self-reference statements combined.

Comments that the child makes about other family members can reveal their pleasures and concerns. Keep in mind that children under the age of 5 or 6 years tend to use very concrete and self-centered terms to describe others in the family (Bigner, 1974). Especially when talking about siblings, it is typical for children to use more emotional terms than when they talk about their parents or peers. Furthermore, children generally use more unfriendly than friendly terms in describing their siblings, especially when they are young. Interestingly, youngsters are usually more sophisticated and elaborate in their descriptions of aspects that they do not like about their brothers or sisters. They are also likely to see any behavior or characteristic resulting in direct, personal benefit as the siblings' strengths (e.g., "He makes me ice cream").

When analyzing the Sibling Role Play Assessment, children's description of each person should be categorized separately in order to examine any trends in the way in which they perceive particular family members. Therefore, for each family member, you would categorize the child's comments as positive, negative, and general—using similar guidelines as with the self-references. Positive comments about a brother might include statements such as, "Tom has the greatest wheelchair. You should see how fast he goes on it" and, "My brother is always so happy to see me in the morning when he wakes up." Negative comments about a sister would include, "My sister has ugly grey teeth" and, "My sister will never learn how to ride a bicycle." General statements about family members often include neutral descriptions of appearance and daily activities, such as, "My mother works at the supermarket" or, "My father doesn't eat his salad." Again, a ratio of positive, negative, and general comments about a particular family member against all comments regarding that family member can be compared before and after the workshop series.

EVALUATION OF SIBLING BEHAVIOR AT HOME

In one project (Lobato, 1981, 1985) in which the young Sibling Workshop Series was implemented, parents standardized their observations of the children together at home. For most children, the type and amount of contact that they had with their brother or sister remained the same throughout the course of the workshops, and improvements were documented by a few parents. Though obser-

vations of the siblings at home on a regular basis would provide a great deal of information about the children's relationship, this would constitute an unrealistic intrusion into family life. A reasonable alternative to outside observers might be to encourage parents to maintain an ongoing log about conversations that they have with their child during the course of the workshop series or observations that they make of the siblings together. Also, parents can take "snapshot" notes on their children's interactions on an intermittent, predetermined schedule. With such a technique, parents could establish particular times of each day to observe their children's ongoing activity. At the determined times only, parents would jot down what the children are doing and whether the emotional tone of their interactions are positive, negative, or neutral. This type of system is less time consuming and biased than an ongoing log because the parents' decision to record their observations would be determined by a clock. With an ongoing log, parents may end up making entries of only very significant or memorable sibling interactions—those that attract their attention. Though these are very interesting indeed, they may not provide a representative sample of the way in which the children interact throughout the day. Other, more mundane and typical interactions could be ignored. By scheduling the time of the observations beforehand, a more representative sample may be obtained.

SUMMARY

In order for group services for young siblings to survive, there must be evidence that the program is effective and enjoyable. Though you probably won't be able to prove that the Sibling Workshop Series made a permanent impact on the children and families, you should be able to evaluate selected aspects of the program's effect. The most essential piece of information for the future survival of the program is the consumer satisfaction data that is collected from the parents. Fortunately, parent feedback is relatively easy to obtain. In contrast, demonstrations of the effects of the Sibling Workshop Series on the siblings themselves is much more time consuming. Decisions regarding evaluation techniques should be made prior to beginning any series so that ample comparisons can be made of the children before and after their participation. The evaluation techniques that you select should be systematic and unbiased for program administration and funding purposes. However, they should also be flexible and sensitive enough to the children and families who are participating so that the information that they provide can be used to improve their experiences with the program.

CHAPTER 9

EXPLAINING MEDICAL
AND
DEVELOPMENTAL
PROBLEMS

BEGINNING HONEST CONVERSATIONS ABOUT A DIFFICULT topic at an early age will not make a problem disappear, but will provide the child with a clear message that problems can be discussed and shared within the family. Many people agree, in theory, that young siblings deserve some information and honesty about their brothers or sisters, yet they often are uncertain as to how, when, and what information should be provided. Parents want to be able to encourage an open atmosphere at home in which children feel that they can share their concerns as well as their delights, but they do not know how to do so. Furthermore, parents do not want to overlook their siblings' own needs in the process of caring for their child with a chronic illness or disability. However, the reality is that it is often difficult to balance the needs of young brothers and sisters with the needs of a child with significant medical and developmental problems.

The purpose of this chapter is to provide guidelines for encouraging open communication within the family and for explaining medical and developmental problems to young brothers and sisters. Also included in this chapter are techniques used to balance brothers' and sisters' needs for information with their needs for developing their own interests and identity.

GUIDELINES FOR ENCOURAGING OPEN COMMUNICATION

Young children learn the rules about family discussion by observing and listening to their parents and other family members. Young children are naturally curious and accepting of whatever appears to be accepted by the adults around them. If young siblings see and hear other family members talk about a child's disability or illness honestly and calmly, they will eventually learn to do the same. If they are encouraged to ask questions or express their confusion about medical or developmental problems and if the responses that they receive are simple and sincere, then their understanding of their brother's or sister's condition will mature in a healthy, adaptive direction. However, if young siblings' concerns or comments are met only with uncontrolled emotions or misinformation, then their opportunities for understanding will be limited. They will only be able to rely on their immature interpretations of what they overhear and imagine. They will miss out on the hard-earned wisdom that the adults around them have accrued.

Even children as young as 3 years of age can recognize some of their brothers' and sisters' problems, especially when they have contact with many different children and their brothers and sisters are older than they. Three years old generally is not too young to share comments about a child's disability or illness. With young preschoolers, take the opportunity to explain other children's behavior and feelings or to explain the family routine (or lack of routine). Do this in relation to healthy, normally developing children, as well as the child with an illness or disability. This will help the preschooler understand people, in general, and their brother or sister, in specific. By taking advantage of daily opportunities to practice explaining other's behavior, it won't seem so odd or sensitive when you also explain the behavior or routines of the child with special needs.

As children mature, their understanding of and experience with a brother's or sister's condition changes. The door to conversation must remain open even after a child appears to have acquired a good understanding of the problem. Because the implications of the problem change periodically, brothers and sisters will have new questions and challenges to face as they grow older. For example, young siblings are concerned with the frequent absences from their parents, while older children may become more concerned with the reactions of other children when their brother or sister enters school. Furthermore, during their middle childhood and teenage years, many siblings begin to grapple with the question of who will take care of the child when their parents are no longer able.

Siblings, themselves, often present the opportunity to talk by asking a question about a brother or sister or some aspect of the family routine. The child's specific question should be answered as directly as possible. Additional information or comments should be offered only for as long as the child appears interested. If the child's attention wanders, end the discussion by praising the child and encouraging other questions in the future. For example, "Well, I'm glad you asked me about Nicky's doctor visit. Sometimes all this business is confusing for me too. Whenever there's something you want to know about Nicky, make sure you remember to ask."

Be willing to admit the personally frustrating or confusing aspects of the child's problem in the sibling's presence. This occasional admission of frustration will provide siblings with a verbal model of one way to cope when they are feeling bad. These comments should not involve complaining about the child as a person or in any way communicating that the child is loved any less. Such comments should be limited to frustrations with the disease or disability, not the child. For example, at the end of a tough interaction, you might comment to a brother or sister:

You know, I wish that Johnny did not have to take this medicine so much. I know that he doesn't like it because he always fights with me when it's time to get it. Even though I know that he is not trying to get me mad when I give it to him, sometimes his struggling so hard makes me feel angry. We are going to have to figure out a good way to get him to take his medicine more easily so that everybody feels better. Are there ever times when you feel a bit frustrated like me?

Some parents feel uneasy with the idea of expressing negative reactions about a child with an illness or disability because it feels like an unfair betrayal of an innocent person. However, when these comments are occasional in comparison to how freely positive reactions are expressed, then siblings can learn that they have an outlet for verbally expressing negative feelings within the family. They may not as readily keep feelings building up inside.

When you do not understand something about the illness or disability, be honest and say so. Suggest how or where you could all get more information. If interest in the information continues, then pursue the answer together (e.g., go to the library together).

Sometimes children are reluctant to talk about their brothers and sisters even though parents are encouraging open communication. Some children can be encouraged to talk by reading children's books about related subjects. A list of books for young children about a variety of medical and developmental problems appears in the Annotated Bibliography at the end of the book. If the text of a particular book does not quite capture what you want to express, then consider modifying the text, especially if the sibling is not yet ready to read. Sometimes it is easier to begin talking about children other than the sibling's own brother or sister. The photographs and illustrations in the books can provide a good point of departure.

Similarly, when you are out with the child in the community or are visiting a special classroom or clinic related to the other child's care, encourage communication about the settings and people that you see there. If your child does not volunteer any comments, then volunteer some of your own honest thoughts. For example, you might comment to your child, "Gee, it looks like that little girl over there is around your age. She seems to be waiting here too, like us, while her sister sees the doctor. I wonder what she's thinking while she sits there?"

Do not confuse open communication about a child's illness or disability with an obsession about the problem. The goal is to encourage young children to ask questions and to share experiences when they need to, not to neglect all the other aspects of their lives as children. Young brothers and sisters need a broad range of experiences with their families and friends. If a child has many interesting and exciting experiences, he or she will naturally want to talk about them. These comments and long, drawn out stories should

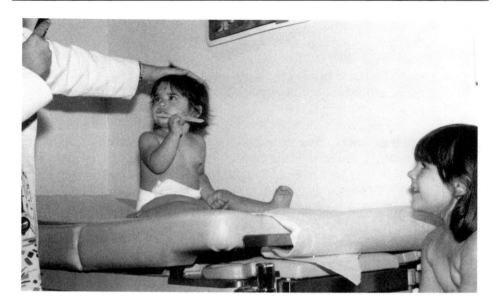

be listened to with as much intensity and enthusiasm as the child's comments about his or her brother or sister. You need to communicate that you are interested in your child as a little person with his or her own developing identity by listening. If you show more intense interest in his or her comments about disabilities or illnesses than any other topic, you could stifle the child's development in other more important areas.

Sometimes siblings, themselves, seem too involved or obsessed with their brothers' or sisters' problems. They gain attention by being very good helpers and neglecting other aspects of their own development. They say that they don't want to go out with other children because that would leave their brother or sister alone, or they want to keep their mother company and help her take care of the child. They begin to feel as if they are little adults with few emotional needs of their own. If this pattern begins to develop, it is important to act quickly to correct it, regardless of how much of a relief the child's participation in the household routine provides. Plan a regular time with that child out of the house and follow through on these plans even if he or she protests. Set aside time with the healthy sibling(s) alone on a regular basis, even if it is only 15 minutes every day. Announce that conversation about any aspect of the other child's problems will be off limits during that period. Treat this time with the sibling(s) as sacred. If you do not have another responsible person to watch your ill or disabled child during this time, then you must try to teach that child that this is a rest period for him or her as well. If your child with the illness or disability is not accustomed to a rest alone, then gradually work your way up from

very brief periods of time alone to about 15 minutes. Do not abandon your attempts to provide siblings with undivided attention if
your child who is ill or disabled cries or has a tantrum when left
alone for these brief periods. As long as the child is in a safe environment, ignore his or her appeals for attention and turn your devotion
to your other child(ren).

Sometimes siblings feel more comfortable talking with other
children about their concerns regarding their brothers' or sisters'
problems. Encourage the clinics or agencies that you and your child
are involved with to establish programs and groups for brothers and
sisters. Chapter 5 describes the range of services that have developed thus far for brothers and sisters. Become familiar with these
services and advocate that they become part of your family's provided options.

GLOSSARY OF DEFINITIONS OF MEDICAL AND
DEVELOPMENTAL PROBLEMS SUITABLE FOR YOUNG SIBLINGS

Definitions or explanations of a variety of significant childhood illnesses and disabilities are presented in terms that are appropriate
for children generally between the ages of 3 and 8 years. The explanations can be modified to match the context of either a parent-child
or leader-child relationship. They are worded as though a parent or
leader were speaking directly with a young sibling or group of
siblings.

Guidelines for Developing
Definitions of Medical and Developmental Terms

Because the list presented may not be all inclusive, follow the
guidelines below to construct your own definition. Practice or rehearse your definition with people who are knowledgeable about
the disorder and who understand young children.

1. A statement should be made of the major part(s) of the body
    that is involved. Though many conditions affect numerous
    organ systems, concentrate on the one or two systems that
    are primarily affected.
2. A statement of the functional significance of the condition is
    important. Young children understand best what they can see
    and what children can do. Include in any explanation exam-
    ples of the ways in which the children's appearance and move-
    ments may or may not be affected. However, be careful not to
    limit the functional possibilities associated with any particular
    condition.

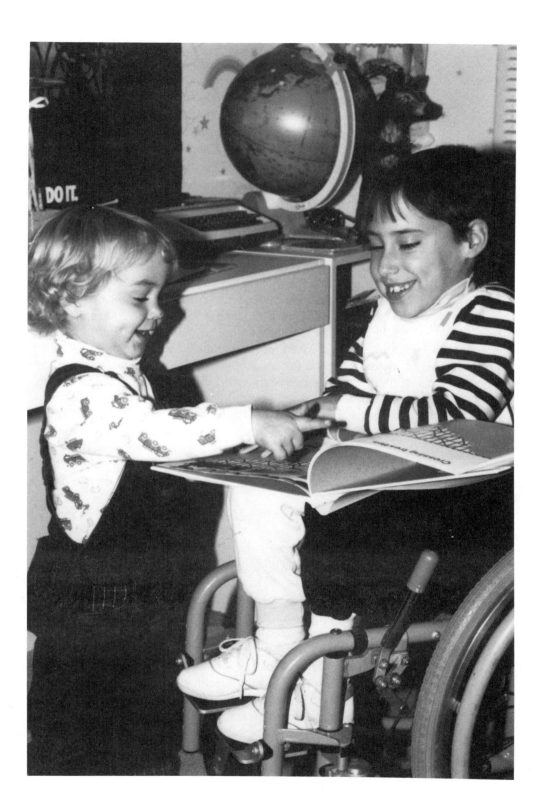

3. It is crucial to provide reassurance that the condition is not contagious and that the sibling him- or herself is healthy and perfectly normal. Because etiology, or the cause, of a problem is often very complicated and may be based on knowledge of abstract aspects such as heredity or cell structure, it is often of limited value to very young children. In fact, in the case of inherited disorders, very young children are easily confused by the fact that there are diseases that you can "get" from your parents but are not contagious. As children mature they become more capable of understanding biological and abstract causes of diseases and disabilities. Indepth discussions of genetics are usually more productive after their preschool and early elementary school years.

4. A statement that the sibling was not responsible for the child's condition must be included. Even though it may be obvious to adults that the sibling had nothing to do with a child's disability or illness, this is a rather common misconception among young siblings. Therefore, an explicit comment that the sibling is not responsible for causing the problem is always warranted.

5. If there is more than one word in the professional or lay vocabulary to describe the condition, let the child know of them. Do not be bashful about saying street words and explaining what people mean by them. Though you may have a strong preference for a particular word or phrase, and find others offensive, young children will probably be better able to cope with whatever they hear from others if you prepare them for it in advance.

6. Try to focus on the strengths and abilities of the individual child.

7. An optimistic statement about current treatment and ongoing research should also be offered. Though a cure is not available for many chronic conditions, it is comforting for youngsters to understand that treatments and research are ongoing. In those cases where treatments resemble cures (e.g., as in PKU), this should be emphasized so that hope can be maintained. The mistake should not be made, however, of suggesting that a child is likely to grow out of a condition that is highly likely to persist throughout his or her lifetime. Because of their immature concepts of time, young siblings can have difficulty understanding specific time frames. It is easy for them to think that everything will get better with enough time or treatment. It is very appropriate to admit to a child that adults cannot predict how a particular child will do with time and treatment. It is usually comforting to the youngster to follow such a statement with a comment about doing the best possible to make everyone's future the brightest possible.

The disabilities and chronic illnesses listed below are presented in alphabetical order.

AIDS or Human Immunodeficiency Virus

AIDS is a disease, something that makes people very sick. AIDS comes from a virus that doctors call the HIV virus (the human immunodeficiency virus). Mostly adults get AIDS, but sometimes babies are born with AIDS because their mothers had the virus in their own blood when they were pregnant. Other boys and girls have become sick with AIDS after they had an operation and were given extra blood that doctors didn't know had the HIV virus in it. When babies or children have AIDS they get sick alot because their bodies are very weak and can't fight bad germs. Doctors believe that you cannot get AIDS from your brother or sister by playing together or eating together or doing any of the usual things you do together. Doctors do say that brothers and sisters should be careful not to get their blood on each other, though. Right now there is no cure for AIDS—there is no medicine that makes the sickness go away. Doctors and nurses can give medicines that help children feel better for awhile and many people are working hard to find a cure.

Asthma

Asthma is a problem that children and adults can have. It is a problem with breathing. If somebody has asthma, they have trouble breathing air in and out smoothly, like this. (Demonstrate) Instead, it is hard for them to get a nice deep breath. When people have asthma, they wheeze a lot when they breathe. Wheezing sounds like this. (Demonstrate) It can be very scary to have trouble breathing. There are special medicines that help asthma. Most of the time you take the medicine at home, but sometimes the asthma gets so bad that the person goes to the hospital to take the medicine. Some children get their asthma problems, or have "asthma attacks," when they smell certain things or get near furry animals. But when those things aren't there, the children are perfectly fine and can run and jump and do all the great things that you do without having a problem breathing. You won't catch asthma from your brother or sister, but sometimes a few people in the same family have asthma. Then everybody in the family has to help everybody else get rid of the things that make them sick (e.g., dust and furry animals) and they can help each other with the medicine when they need it.

Attention Deficit-Hyperactivity Disorder

Right now, while I am talking, you are sitting pretty still and are listening to what I am saying. You are paying attention to me and I am paying attention to you. Sometimes, children and adults have trouble paying attention or sitting still, like they can't watch a whole commercial on television. They sometimes are too active. That's what hyperactive means—too active or super active. Well, if children have a lot of trouble paying attention to important things and people, then they can have attention deficit or hyperactivity disorder. This problem makes it hard for the children to learn in school and to obey their parents at home. A lot of times, children with hyperactivity need to get extra help at school and at home to do better. Sometimes their doctors give them a medicine to help this problem.

Everybody has trouble paying attention or sitting still once in awhile. This happens for a lot of different reasons and can happen every day. We only call it by a big fancy name like attention deficit-hyperactivity disorder when the problem just won't go away or when it is hard for the child to learn in school. There is nothing you did or do that makes your brother or sister hyperactive and you cannot catch it from him or her.

Autism or Pervasive Developmental Disorder

Autism is something that is very hard to explain because adults do not know a whole lot about it either. Some people also use the words "pervasive developmental disorder" when they are talking about problems like autism. So, if you hear those words, you'll know that they're talking about a similar problem. People say that a child has autism when he or she learns and acts very differently from other children. Children who have autism often do not look at people when people look at them. Children with autism have a lot of trouble learning how to talk to people and often cannot understand what they say. Some children with autism never learn how to talk at all. Other children learn how to say words but do not always know what they mean and say certain words over and over again, even when they don't make sense. Some boys and girls who have autism do things that other children think look strange because they do them when everybody else is doing something different. Like, maybe they're walking back and forth while everybody else is playing a game together. Sometimes they just keep doing it over and over again when most children would have stopped or become bored. They may also look at their hands or spin the wheel of a toy car over and over again. It is hard to play games with a child who has autism. Sometimes brothers and sisters make up their own special little games that only they play together.

We don't know exactly why children end up with autism. What we think is that something is probably wrong with the way their brains work. You know that the brain inside of your head helps you learn and get along with people. It also helps you learn how to talk, when to talk, and when to be happy or sad. When children have autism, it may be because their brains have trouble learning to do those things, but there can be other ones that they do very well. Even though we don't know what makes autism happen, we do know that brothers or sisters can't give it to each other.

Autism is something that usually does not go away. It is probably there when the children are babies, and stays there when they become adults. There are special ways of teaching children who have autism so that they learn to do as much as they can without help. Scientists and teachers are learning new ways of helping children with autism, and they are trying to find ways to make sure that autism does not happen.

Blindness (see Vision Problems)

Cancer (see Hodgkin's Disease, Leukemia, Neuroblastoma, Wilm's Tumor)

There are many different kinds of sicknesses called "cancer." Many people get scared when they hear that word because they think people always die from cancer. But that is not true. There are some kinds of cancer that doctors and nurses can make go away completely so that the children can grow up to be healthy again. The word "cancer" by itself means that something inside the body is growing wrong. Sometimes it's part of the blood. Sometimes it's inside the eye. Sometimes it's on the inside of the brain. When a child has cancer, he or she will need to spend a lot of time going to doctors and special hospitals to get better. They have to go there with one of their parents, so mothers and fathers have to spend a lot of time outside of the house. It isn't easy for anybody when that happens to families, is it? Very special medicines and other treatments are given at the hospital and at home for a few years. Sometimes the medicine gives the boys and girls really bad stomach aches or makes their hair fall out or makes them very tired all the time, but they have to take the medicine anyway so that the cancer goes away.

We don't know why some children get cancer, but we do know that you can't catch it from your brother or sister. We also know that you could not have given it to him or her. We are glad that you are healthy and that doctors and nurses and scientists are finding new ways to take care of children with cancer, too.

Cerebral Palsy (see Developmental Delay or Mental Retardation, Developmental Disability, Handicapped or Disabled)

Cerebral palsy is a word used to talk about problems that some children have with moving the muscles in their bodies. Some people also call it CP. You might also hear words like diplegia and hemi-paresis or spastic. These are all big words that are part of cerebral palsy or CP. To understand cerebral palsy, you have to think about the brain inside of your head. Your brain is the very important part of your body that makes everything else in your body do the right things at the right time. So, when you are sitting here, your brain helps your ears to hear, it helps your eyes to see, and it helps your hands to stay still or to move when you want them to. Sometimes when a baby is born or right after the baby is born, the baby's brain gets hurt. Sometimes the brain gets better but sometimes it doesn't. When the brain gets hurt, it can't help all of the other parts of the body do what they are supposed to do. That's what cerebral palsy is. Sometimes the brain can't help the muscles in the legs so the child's legs are either too stiff or too weak or maybe the child's legs move when the child doesn't want them to. But this boy or girl might be able to move his or her arms just fine because his or her brain is still helping the arms. Other children who have cerebral palsy, or CP, really can't move any part of their bodies and that can be very hard. Some children who have CP have only very little problems. Most of the time these boys and girls don't have any trouble doing what other children do. Some need special equipment to help them move, like braces on their legs or wheelchairs. If they have cerebral palsy really bad, then they usually have to see a lot of doctors, teachers, and special therapists. They have to do many exercises to do their best. Sometimes mothers and fathers have to help them move their arms and legs so that they don't get stuck in one spot. Some boys and girls with CP learn how to walk, but some others always need wheelchairs because they never learn how to walk.

Babies can end up with CP for many different reasons. Some-times it's because the baby was born too early and was too small. Sometimes it's because the baby had trouble breathing right when it was born. Sometimes we don't know why it happens, but we do know that brothers and sisters can't make it happen to their new babies. We also know that they can't catch it from the new baby or from an older brother or sister who has it. Right now there is no way to make cerebral palsy go away, but there are doctors, scientists, teachers, and therapists who are doing the best they can to learn more about CP and how to make it better.

Cleft Lip and Cleft Palate

A cleft lip or a cleft palate is something that a baby is born with. Nothing you or your mother or father did caused it to happen. It just happens every once in awhile. A cleft lip is when the baby's top lip has an extra space or opening. The lip isn't smooth like yours.

Sometimes a space is open from the lip to the nose. You can see a baby's cleft lip right when the baby is born and that makes the baby look different. A cleft lip makes it hard for a baby to drink. Doctors can fix the baby's lip and nose in the hospital when the baby is still very tiny. After the doctors fix the baby's lip, it is easier to feed the baby. Then when the babies grow up, they have a small scar on their lips and can do everything that everyone else does.

Your palate is on the inside of your mouth. It's the top of your mouth, the roof of your mouth behind your teeth. Look to where I am pointing in my mouth. That's my palate. Now you point to your palate. Good. If a baby has a cleft palate, then that part of his or her mouth didn't grow right before he or she was born. There would be a space or opening in the palate, in the roof of the mouth. Cleft palates make it hard for babies to eat and talk right. Doctors can fix the baby's cleft palate a little bit at a time. By the time they grow up, they will have small scars where their mouths were fixed. Sometimes children will need extra help eating and learning how to talk. Boys and girls who have cleft palates when they were babies turn into kids who talk and eat and do everything you do.

Cystic Fibrosis

Cystic fibrosis is a problem that a baby can be born with. Sometimes there will be a few babies or children with cystic fibrosis in the same family. You know what mucus is, even though you might not always call it that? Mucus is the stuff in your nose and throat that keeps your nose and throat kind of wet. If you get a cold, sometimes you end up with a lot of mucus and have to blow your nose and cough to get it out. Well, there is also mucus in other parts of your body that you can't see, like your lungs. When you breathe in air, it goes down into your lungs. See, when your lungs fill up like a balloon with nice clean air, that part of your body gets bigger and you breathe. When somebody has cystic fibrosis, there is always too much mucus. The mucus can get stuck in the lungs and make it very hard to breathe. It isn't the same as a cold, even though you have a lot of mucous with a cold and with cystic fibrosis. A cold goes away after a short time and there's no more extra mucus. With cystic fibrosis, though, the extra mucus never goes away completely. It gets worse as the child gets older. Sometimes children with CF (that's another way of saying cystic fibrosis) need to eat special foods and take pills. They have to get checked by the doctors a lot and sometimes stay awhile in the hospital if they get really sick. People who have CF usually do not live to be as old as other people, but there is a lot that we are learning about CF to make everybody's life healthier. There's nothing you did (or your parents) that made the CF happen and you cannot catch it from your brother or sister. It is wonderful that you do not have cystic fibrosis. We hope that someday there will be no more CF and that all babies will be born healthy.

Deafness (see Hearing Problems)

Developmental Delay or Mental Retardation (see Cerebral Palsy, Developmental Disability, Handicapped or Disabled, Spina Bifida)

When a child has a developmental delay, it means that they are developing or learning slowly. The word "delayed" means that something is taking longer to happen. Children develop, or grow, into adults. They develop from babies who can't talk or walk yet into adults and children like you who can do so many different things. It only took you about four or five, or maybe six, years to learn everything you know. If a child has a developmental delay or mental retardation, it will take a much longer time for the child to learn. Sometimes they don't learn everything you learn by the time they grow up, but they can learn a lot. If your brother or sister has a developmental delay, maybe you also hear people say that he or she has mental retardation, too. The words are different, but they can mean the same thing—that the child learns slower than other children. Someday you might hear somebody call another person a "retard." It might hurt your feelings to hear the word "retarded" used like a bad word. People who use the word "retard" like that do not really know what it means. When we say the word "retarded" or use the words "mental retardation," we mean the same thing as the words "slower" or "delayed." There are a lot of reasons why some children are slow or have developmental delays. For some children, special teachers and doctors can make the delay go away. But, for many others, they will always need special doctors and teachers. We are very happy that most children are healthy and learn as easily as you do. That makes you special. But many people are working hard so that other boys and girls won't have to have developmental delays.

Developmental Disability (see Cerebral Palsy, Developmental Delay or Mental Retardation, Handicapped or Disabled, Spina Bifida)

When a child has a disability, it means that he or she has a problem doing something important. When it is a developmental disability, it means that the child has trouble developing or growing up and learning. Children develop or grow into adults. They develop from babies who can't talk or walk yet into adults and children like you who can do so many things. There are many different kinds of developmental disabilities. Some boys and girls have trouble learning some things but are fine with others. For example, there are children who have trouble moving their legs, but are really smart and can do puzzles with a lot of pieces. There also are children who have developmental disabilities who have trouble doing a lot of important things. You might hear people say that your brother or sister has a developmental disability. You might also hear people say that he or she is handicapped or has mental retardation, cerebral palsy, or spina bifida (Note: Say only the ones that apply. Refer to all other explanations.).

Diabetes

Diabetes is a problem that children and adults can have. Diabetes happens when the body has trouble using food the right way. Everybody has a special kind of "sugar," the kind that gives us energy. It isn't like the sugar you put on cereal, though. It looks different. There is something else inside the body that helps the sugar move around—that is called insulin. Insulin moves the sugar to wherever it needs to go in the body. When somebody has diabetes, the insulin can't move the sugar where it should go and the person can't get energy the right way. All the sugar builds up in the body and the person gets sick. It can be scary when children get sick from diabetes because they can get very weak and can't eat or think right. Luckily, we know just what to do to make it better so they won't get sick too many times.

Even though we don't know exactly why some children get diabetes and others don't, a lot of times a couple of the people in the family will have it. You can't catch diabetes from your brother or sister and you didn't give it to him or her. We don't have a way of making it go away forever, but we do have ways of making it much better. Boys and girls who have diabetes have to be careful about what they eat. They can't have too much sugar because it will make them sick. They need to be especially careful when they do extra exercise or run around a lot. Most children who have diabetes have to get injections or shots every day. The shots have that stuff called insulin in them. They put extra insulin in since their bodies don't have enough without the shot. The extra insulin they put in helps move all the sugar around and gives the child's body the energy it needs.

There are scientists, doctors, and nurses who are looking for ways to "cure" diabetes, to make it go away, and there are doctors and nurses who are learning ways to make it better and better. If that can happen, children who have diabetes can be just as healthy as you are.

Down Syndrome (see Developmental Delay or Mental Retardation)

There are many babies born every year who have Down syndrome. Those are words we use to describe children whose bodies are a little bit different than yours or mine. Boys and girls who have Down syndrome look like other children in most ways, but look like each other in special ways, too. Sometimes they are smaller than other children their age and their eyes are shaped a little different than our eyes. Children who have Down syndrome grow and learn slower than others. Most children who have Down syndrome have mental retardation and learn slower. They like to learn the same things you like to learn, though, like riding bikes and writing with markers. They can get extra help to learn how to talk and read in school.

We don't know why some babies have Down syndrome. It is just something that happens. Nothing you did caused it to happen. Just because your brother or sister has Down syndrome doesn't mean that you have it or will catch it. We can't make Down syndrome go away, but people are learning a lot about it so that maybe it won't happen to as many babies.

Epilepsy (see Seizure Disorders or Epilepsy)

Handicapped or Disabled (see Cerebral Palsy, Developmental Delay or Mental Retardation, Developmental Disability)

The word "handicapped" just means that somebody needs extra help doing something. Some people say the word "disabled" to mean the same thing as handicapped. If a child has a handicap or has a disability, they can have a problem with their eyes or legs or any other part of their body. A person who needs a wheelchair has a handicap and someone who needs a hearing aid has a handicap, too. Even though their problems are different, the word "handicapped" or "disabled" can be used for both. The words "handicapped" and "disabled" do not tell us the kind of problem that the child has or the kind of help he or she needs.

Sometimes we know what causes a handicap and sometimes we don't. For all children, though, we like to find out what kind of help they need and then we like to give them that help. Just like with you, even though you do not have a handicap or a disability, you need help with things sometimes—like tying your shoes or putting a braid in your hair. When you need help, adults like to give you help, too. As you get older, you learn to do more and more for yourself. The same happens with boys and girls who have handicaps or disabilities. Sometimes disabilities can go away but sometimes they do not. As the children get older, though, they learn to do more and more for themselves, just like you. Even though they have trouble doing some activities, there will be others that they do without any trouble at all. Handicaps are not things that you can catch from another person, so you won't get it from your brother or sister, and he or she didn't get it from you.

Hearing Problems

While we are sitting here talking, there are many sounds all around us. Can you tell me some of the sounds that you hear? Yes, you can hear me talking and I can hear you talking. We can hear the cars outside and the birds making noise. If we listen carefully, we can also hear real small sounds like my watch ticking and somebody's television in the other room. Well, our ears are what we hear with. If you put your hands over your ears, you can't hear all of the different sounds, can you? Sometimes one ear or both ears don't work quite right. Sometimes the ears hear loud sounds like cars okay, but can't hear quiet ones like clocks. Some people really cannot hear much of anything at all. The word "deaf" means not being able to hear anything. If a baby is deaf, the baby will have trouble learning how to talk because he or she will not be able to hear other people talking. The baby will only see other people's mouths moving, but won't hear the people's voices. There are special things called hearing aids that help some children and adults hear better. The hearing aids are so small that boys and girls can wear them in their ears. The hearing aids can make sounds louder. If the hearing aid still can't make sounds loud enough for the child to learn how to talk, he or she can learn a special way of "talking" with hands. They put their hands and fingers in different positions for different words. This is called sign language. The hands make "signs" that other people can look at and understand. It takes time to learn how to use sign language. A special teacher can teach sign language to children and parents who need to learn it. People have trouble hearing for lots of different reasons. Nothing you did made your brother or sister have trouble hearing.

Hodgkin's Disease (see Cancer)

Hodgkin's disease is a kind of cancer in very small parts of somebody's body. It is something you can't really see with your eyes but you can tell when the person has it because they get a lot of fevers and lose weight. Sometimes they get sweaty at night and get itchy all over their bodies. Most of the time when children get fevers or get itchy they don't have Hodgkin's disease. When children have Hodgkin's disease they go to special doctors and nurses in hospitals. Most of the time their mother and father goes with them. In the hospital, there are special medicines and special machines or equipment that make the disease go away. Sometimes these medicines give the children stomach aches and make them feel very tired or make their hair fall out. These boys and girls have to take the medicine, though, so that they can get better. After they go to the hospital, the children come home and take more medicine. Sometimes they have to stay home from school for a long time and teachers come to the house instead.

Nothing you did made your brother or sister get Hodgkin's disease and you can't get it or catch it from him or her either. We are glad that there are ways that doctors and nurses can help make the disease go away, then all boys and girls can be healthy like you.

Hyperactivity (see Attention Deficit-Hyperactivity Disorder)

Juvenile Rheumatoid Arthritis

The rheumatoid arthritis that children get is also called JRA by some people. JRA stands for juvenile rheumatoid arthritis. We don't know what causes it, but we do know that brothers and sisters can't give it to each other. Joints are these parts of your body—like your knuckles, your neck, your elbows, and knees. When boys and girls have arthritis, their joints hurt. Sometimes the joints hurt so much that it becomes very hard to move the part that hurts. If it gets really bad, they may not be able to go to school and have to rest and take medicine to make the pain go away. When the arthritis is bad, it might be hard to ride a bicycle or to even write with a pencil. People who have JRA should do special exercises to keep their bodies moving easily. For example, if a girl has arthritis in her knees, then she will do leg exercises to keep her knees bending. (Demonstrate) The medicines that doctors use help a little bit, but don't make the arthritis go away. There are scientists and other doctors, though, who are trying to find other medicines that make these boys and girls feel better.

Learning Disabilities

There are many different kinds of learning disabilities. Some children have trouble learning how to read. Some children have trouble learning how to write. Others who have learning disabilities have trouble learning and remembering how to count and do other things with numbers. Children who have learning disabilities can be smart in many other ways besides ones that are a problem. For example, they can read well but have trouble remembering telephone numbers or are great swimmers or divers but have trouble reading. When somebody has a lot of trouble learning to read, sometimes people say the boy and girl has dyslexia. Most of the time, nobody really understands why some people have learning disabilities. It can make them feel bad, especially in school, because the work is hard for them and easier for other boys and girls. There's nothing you did to cause your brother's or sister's trouble in school. Just because he or she needs extra help doesn't mean that you will need it, too. We are glad that there are special teachers in school to give boys and girls the extra help they need.

Leukemia (see Cancer)

Leukemia is when there is something very wrong with somebody's blood. Because blood moves through all parts of the body, the problem can go to parts like the bones. You can't see leukemia with your eyes, but children show other signs of leukemia like having a fever for a long time, getting big bruises easily, and getting bruises that take a long time to go away. These will be very different from the bruises you get because you are healthy and you do not have leukemia. Sometimes boys and girls even say that their bones hurt. When doctors do special tests, they can tell that someone has leukemia. Once they find it, there are very good ways to take care of it. There are special medicines to give and other treatments to do in the hospital that can make most children completely better. Sometimes these medicines give the boys and girls stomach aches and make them feel very tired, but they have to take the medicines anyway because it makes the leukemia go away. Doctors usually want either the mother or father to stay with the child in the hospital to help him or her get better. After the children come home from the hospital, they still take their medicines. They might go back to the doctors a lot and can't go to school all the time. It isn't easy for anybody when somebody gets leukemia in a family.

We are very glad that you are healthy. You cannot catch leukemia from your brother or sister. Nothing you did or your mother and father did made your brother or sister get the leukemia, either. We are also very happy that there are medicines that can help him or her get better.

Mental Retardation (see Developmental Delay or Mental Retardation)

Muscular Dystrophy

Muscular dystrophy is a big word that is hard for some people to say. So sometimes people just call it MD. Muscular dystrophy or MD is a problem with somebody's muscles. The muscles in your body are what make you strong. Your muscles in your legs help you walk and run and go up and down stairs. The muscles in your arms help you pick up and carry things like toys and chairs and glasses of juice.

Usually, as children get older, their muscles grow. The muscles get bigger and stronger. That is what will happen to you since you do not have muscular dystrophy. When people have muscular dystrophy or MD, though, their muscles stop growing. After awhile, their muscles get smaller and weaker instead of bigger and stronger. When the muscles get too small or weak then it becomes harder to walk and run. Special equipment like braces and wheelchairs will help the person move when the muscles cannot do it any more. There is nothing that your parents or you did to make the MD happen to your brother or sister. Also, you cannot catch MD like you catch a cold—you cannot get it from your brother or sister by being near to him or her. There is no cure for MD right now. That means that there is nothing that we can do right now to make the muscular dystrophy go away. Many people like doctors and scientists are working very hard, though, to find a cure—to find a way to make the muscular dystrophy go away.

Neuroblastoma (see Cancer)

Neuroblastoma is a kind of cancer. When a baby or a child has neuroblastoma they have a tumor or something growing inside the body where it should not be. The tumor can be very small and is hard to see or feel, but sometimes doctors and nurses can feel it when they give children check-ups. Special tests will tell the doctor when somebody has neuroblastoma. Once the doctor finds the tumor, they will try to take it out by doing a special operation. Then they give other medicine and use special machines to try to make the tumors go away completely. This happens in a hospital and the child's mother or father may stay in the hospital to help the doctors and nurses make their boy or girl better. Once the child can come home, he or she will still need to visit the doctor a lot and will still have to take the medicines. Sometimes the medicines make the child's hair fall out and give him or her stomach aches so that they don't feel good, but they have to take the medicine anyway because we want the tumor to go away. We want them to be healthy, like you. There is nothing that you did or your mother and father did that made the tumor happen. Just because your brother or sister has one does not mean that you will get a tumor, too.

Pervasive Developmental Disorder
(see Autism or Pervasive Developmental Disorder)

Phenylketonuria (PKU) (see Developmental Delay or Mental Retardation)

Phenylketonuria or PKU is a problem that babies are born with. Their bodies use food in a different way than other babies. Babies and children who have PKU need to eat special kinds of food so that they can grow up right. If they do not eat the special foods, they will not grow up right. They will have a lot of problems learning and will become mentally retarded. But, if they eat only the right foods, they will grow up to be just as smart as you are. You cannot catch PKU from being next to your brother or sister. You can even try some of the special food he or she has to eat. But you really cannot give him or her your food without asking your mother or father first. Sometimes it is hard to eat only the special foods, but it is very important. It is really great that we know how to make the PKU better so that boys and girls who have it won't have very bad problems.

Prematurity

When a woman is pregnant—when she is going to have a baby—the baby grows inside of her body for 9 months. It takes 9 whole months for the baby to be big enough and ready to be born. Sometimes babies are born way before the 9 months are up—like when the woman is only 6 or 7 or 8 months pregnant. When the baby is born too early, the baby is premature. Nothing you (or your parents) did caused the baby to be born too early. It was just something that happens every once in awhile.

Premature babies who grow inside their mothers for almost the right amount of time usually do not need a lot of help. They stay in the hospital a few extra days or weeks, but then go home and do fine. But, if the baby was born too, too early the baby will be too, too small. Sometimes those really tiny babies need a lot of extra doctors and nurses in the hospital to help them breathe and eat and grow right. These very, very small babies sometimes stay in the hospital a very long time. Many grow up to be fine like you but other premature babies end up having problems. If they do have problems, then they can get special help for as long as they need it at home and in school.

Seizure Disorders or Epilepsy

Some people call epilepsy a seizure disorder or a seizure problem. Some people even call seizures convulsions or fits. They really mean just about the same thing. Seizures can happen if something goes wrong inside somebody's head, in somebody's brain. The brain is a very important part of your body. It helps you do everything, like breathe, see, move, and talk. When you want to move your hand, your brain tells your hand to move and then tells it to stop. If somebody has a seizure, the brain makes a mistake and the body moves when the person doesn't really want it to. If somebody has a seizure problem, their body can move when they don't want it

to, like their leg or arm moves up and down, up and down or sometimes their whole body shakes and it's not because they are cold
and shivery. Some children don't move around like that but look like
they stop paying attention to what's going on around them. They
look like they might be daydreaming like this. (Demonstrate) These
are all different kinds of seizures. Though it sometimes can be scary
to see somebody have a seizure, you can't catch it. Nothing you did
made the seizure problem happen. Sometimes children who have
epilepsy, who have seizures, feel embarrassed if anyone sees them
when the seizure happens. The good thing is that there are a lot of
different medicines that can help the seizures get better. Sometimes
the medicine turns a big seizure into a smaller one or turns a lot of
seizures into only a couple that happen only once in awhile. Doctors
and nurses and other people are looking for new medicines that
help children with seizures even more.

Sickle Cell Anemia

Sickle cell anemia is something a baby is born with. You cannot
catch it from the baby and he or she did not get it from you. Sometimes a few people in the family will have sickle cell anemia. Sickle
cell anemia is a problem in somebody's blood. Every minute of
every day your body works to make sure you have all the different
things that make new, healthy blood. When people have sickle cell
anemia, their bodies cannot make the blood quite right. Then they
feel tired and weak and sometimes they feel a lot of pain. They hurt
a lot. They can have trouble going to school when they get sick.
There will be times when they feel okay for awhile, then there will
be times when they get sick and hurt again. Right now, there is
nothing we can do to make the sickle cell anemia go away forever.
Doctors, nurses, and other scientists are looking for better medicines to give children with sickle cell anemia so that they can be just
as healthy as you are.

Spina Bifida (see Developmental Disability, Handicapped or Disabled)

Spina bifida is something that babies are born with. Right when they
are born, we can see something wrong with their spines. Your spine
is the part down the middle of your back. (Rub your hand over the
child's spine.) The spine goes from the brain down to the end of
your body here. Your spine is just fine. It grew the way it was supposed to when you were growing inside your mother's body. Your
spine has a bunch of strong bones around a spinal cord. When you
touch your spine or my spine, you can feel the hard bones under
your skin but you cannot feel or see the spinal cord inside the bones.
When babies are born with spina bifida the bones do not cover the

spinal cord right and you can feel and see the cord on the outside of the baby's body. Doctors and nurses have to do operations then to cover up the cord and protect it. The cord is important because it carries messages from the brain to the other parts of the body. When there is something wrong with the cord, like in spina bifida, the messages cannot get through. Even though the child might want to move his or her legs, he or she may not be able to. There are different kinds of spina bifida. Some children can learn how to read and walk and take care of themselves just as well as you do, but other boys and girls will always need help from other people.

We don't know why some babies are born with spina bifida and some are not. It is something that just happens. We know that you cannot catch spina bifida from your brother or sister. We do not have a way of making spina bifida go away completely, but there are ways in which doctors and teachers can help babies with spina bifida to do their best.

Vision Problems

As we sit here talking, there are many things that we both can see. Can you tell me some of the things that you see right now? That's right. We see each other, the couch, and the pillow. Some of the things that we see are very small, like our eyelashes and some things are pretty big, like the door. Some things are very close to us, like our fingers, and some things are very far away, like that car out there. We see with our eyes, don't we? And if you put your hands over your eyes you can't see anything, can you? Sometimes children and adults have trouble seeing because there is something wrong with one or both of their eyes. Some people can only see things that are very close to them, while others can only see things that are far away. Some people cannot see much of anything at all. That's what the word "blind" means—not being able to see anything.

There are a lot of ways to make things easier for children and adults who have trouble seeing. Some people can wear eyeglasses and it makes everything better. Other people need more than eyeglasses. Eyeglasses won't help everybody who can't see. Most of the time, people who have trouble seeing can do most things just fine, like hearing, talking, getting dressed, and things like that, and they can learn how to read books with their hands. There are many books that have the words written in braille. Braille is a special way that words are put on the page, that can be felt by the fingers. Most blind people have no trouble moving around their own houses without seeing, but when they go outside, they might like to take a cane or a seeing eye dog. The cane and the dog help them know when to cross the street and things like that.

Other children have different kinds of problems with their eyes.

For example, some children's eyes cross or do not look at the same thing at the same time. This happens when one part of their eye is stronger than the other. This problem can sometimes get better by covering up the strong eye. That makes the other eye work harder and become stronger—sort of like exercising. Sometimes doctors can do operations in the hospital to make the eye better.

Some babies are born with eye problems. Other people have trouble when they get older. We will check your eyes as you get older to make sure that they stay as healthy as they are right now. You know that nothing you did made your brother or sister have trouble seeing. We are quite happy that there are so many ways to help people with eye problems because then they can see your wonderful smile.

Wilms' Tumor (see Cancer)

Wilms' tumor is a kind of cancer in which there is something wrong inside of somebody's kidney. The kidney is a part of the body that is on the inside. It can't be seen from the outside. A tumor is something that grows in the body in a place where it should not, kind of like a bad lump. The doctors do special tests to find out if someone has Wilms' tumor. If they do have it, then the doctors do an operation in the hospital to take the tumor out. Then the doctor uses special machines and medicines to make sure the children keep getting better. Sometimes this medicine and other things the doctor does gives the boys and girls stomach aches or makes their hair fall out, but they have to keeping taking their medicine because that is what will help make the tumor go away. Even after they come home from the hospital, children who have Wilms' tumor have to go to the doctor a lot. Even though this is not easy on anybody in the family, we are very glad that there are ways in which doctors and nurses can make your brother or sister as healthy as you are. You cannot catch Wilms' tumor from your brother or sister and nothing you did made him or her get it. It is just something that happened. Doctors and scientists are trying to find ways to make sure children always get better from it.

REFERENCES

Abidin, R. (1980). *Parent education and intervention handbook.* Springfield, IL: Charles C Thomas.

Abramovitch, R., Corter, C., & Lando, B. (1979). Sibling interaction in the home. *Child Development, 50,* 997–1003.

Abramovitch, R., Corter, C., & Pepler, D. (1980). Observations of mixed-sex sibling dyads. *Child Development, 51,* 1268–1271.

Abramovitch, R., Pepler, D., & Corter, C. (1982). Patterns of sibling interaction among preschool-age children. In M.E. Lamb & B. Sutton-Smith (Eds.). *Sibling relationships: Their nature and significance across the lifespan* (pp. 61–86). Hillsdale, NJ: Lawrence Erlbaum Associates.

Abramovitch, R., Stanhope, L., Pepler, D., & Corter, C. (1987). The influence of Down's syndrome on sibling interaction. *Journal of Child Psychology and Psychiatry, 28,* 865–879.

August, G.J., Stewart, M.A., & Tsai, L. (1981). The incidence of cognitive disabilities in siblings of autistic children. *British Journal of Psychiatry, 138,* 416–422.

Bank, S., & Kahn, M.D. (1982). *The sibling bond.* New York: Basic Books.

Bedell, J.R., Giordani, B., Amour, J.L., Tavormina, J., & Boll, T. (1977). Life stress and the psychological and medical adjustment of chronically ill children. *Journal of Psychosomatic Research, 21,* 237–242.

Bennett, C.W. (1973). A four-and-a-half year old as a teacher of her hearing impaired sister: A case study. *Journal of Communication Disorders, 6,* 67–75.

Benson, G. (1982, November). *Siblings: Research and implications for family programming.* Paper presented at the annual meeting of The Association for the Severely Handicapped, Denver, CO.

Berstein, D.A., & Borkovec, T.D. (1973). *Progressive relaxation training: A manual for the helping professions.* Champaign, IL: Research Press.

Bibace, R., & Walsh, M. (1980). Development of children's concepts of illness. *Pediatrics, 66,* 912–917.

Bigner, J.A. (1974). A Wernerian developmental analysis of children's descriptions of siblings. *Child Development, 45,* 317–323.

Breslau, N. (1982). Siblings of disabled children: Birth order and age-spacing effects. *Journal of Abnormal Child Psychology, 10,* 85–96.

Breslau, N., Weitzman, M., & Messenger, K. (1981). Psychological functioning of siblings of disabled children. *Pediatrics*, *67*, 344–353.

Brody, G.H., & Stoneman, L. (1986). Contextual issues in the study of sibling socialization. In J.J. Gallagher & P.M. Vietze (Eds.), *Families of handicapped persons: Research, programs, and policy issues* (pp. 197–217). Baltimore: Paul H. Brookes Publishing Co.

Bryant, B.K. (1982). Sibling relationships in middle childhood. In M.E. Lamb & B. Sutton-Smith (Eds.), *Sibling relationships: Their nature and significance across the lifespan* (pp. 87–121). Hillsdale, NJ: Lawrence Erlbaum Associates.

Burbach, D.J., & Peterson, L. (1986). Children's concepts of physical illness: A review and critique of the cognitive-developmental literature. *Health Psychology*, *5*, 307–325.

Byrnes, C., & Love, M. (1983). Sibling day workshops: A wholistic approach. *Sibling Information Network Newsletter*, *2*, 4.

Cairns, N.U., Clark, G.M., Smith, S.D., & Lansky, S.B. (1979). Adaptation of siblings to childhood malignancy. *Journal of Pediatrics*, *3*, 484–487.

Caldwell, B.M., & Guze, G.B. (1960). A study of the adjustment of parents and siblings of institutionalized and noninstitutionalized retarded children. *American Journal of Mental Deficiency*, *64*, 849–861.

Cash, W.M., & Evans, I.N. (1975). Training preschool children to modify their siblings' behavior. *Journal of Behavior Therapy and Experimental Psychiatry*, *6*, 13–16.

Cicirelli, V.G. (1975). Effects of mothers and older siblings on the problem-solving behavior of the younger child. *Developmental Psychology*, *11*, 749–756.

Cleveland, D.W., & Miller, N.B. (1977). Attitudes and life commitments of older siblings of mentally retarded adults: An exploratory study. *Mental Retardation*, *15*, 38–41.

Colletti, G., & Harris, S.L. (1977). Behavior modification in the home: Siblings as behavior modifiers, parents as observers. *Journal of Abnormal Child Psychology*, *5*, 21–30.

Crnic, K.A., Friedrich, W.N., & Greenberg, M.T. (1983). Adaptation of families with mentally retarded children: A model of stress, coping, and family ecology. *American Journal of Mental Deficiency*, *88*, 125–138.

Crnic, K.A., & Leconte, J.M. (1986). Understanding sibling needs and influences. In R.R. Fewell & P.F. Vadasy (Eds.), *Families of handicapped children: Needs and supports across the life span* (pp. 75–98). Austin, TX: PRO-ED.

Daniels, D., Miller, J.J., III, Billings, A.G., & Moos, R.H. (1986). Psychosocial functioning of siblings of children with rheumatic disease. *Journal of Pediatrics*, *109*, 379–383.

Daniels, D., Moos, R.H., Billings, A.G., & Miller, J.J., III. (1987). Psychosocial risk and resistance factors among children with chronic illness, healthy siblings, and healthy controls. *Journal of Abnormal Child Psychology*, *15*, 295–308.

Drotar, D., & Crawford, P. (1985). Psychological adaptation of siblings of chronically ill children: Research and practice implications. *Developmental and Behavioral Pediatrics*, *6*, 355–362.

Dunn, J. (1985). *Sisters and brothers.* Cambridge, MA: Harvard University Press.

Dunn, J., & Kendrick, C. (1982). *Siblings: Love, envy, and understanding.* Cambridge, MA: Harvard University Press.

Dunn, J., Kendrick, C., & MacNamee, R. (1981). The reaction of firstborn children to the birth of a sibling: Mothers' reports. *Journal of Child Psychology and Psychiatry, 22,* 1–18.

Dyson, L.L. (1989). Adjustment of siblings of handicapped children: A comparison. *Journal of Pediatric Psychology, 14,* 215–229.

Fairfield, B. (1983). Workshops for siblings and parents. *Sibling Information Network Newsletter, 2,* 5.

Farber, B. (1959). Effects of a severely mentally retarded child on family integration. *Monographs of the Society for Research in Child Development, 21*(75).

Farber, B. (1960). Family organization and crisis: Maintenance of integration in families with a severely mentally retarded child. *Monographs of the Society for Research in Child Development, 25* (75).

Farber, B. (1963). Interactions with retarded siblings and life goals of children. *Marriage and Family Living, 25,* 96–98.

Farber, B., Jenne, W., & Toigo, R. (1960). Family crisis and the decision to institutionalize the retarded child. *Council for Exceptional Children, Research Monograph Series, A*(1).

Farber, B., & Ryckman, D. (1965). Effects of severely mentally retarded children on family relationships. *Mental Retardation Abstracts, 2,* 1–17.

Farkas, A. (1974). Adaptation of patients, siblings, and mothers to cystic fibrosis (Doctoral dissertation, Michigan State University, 1973). *Dissertation Abstracts International, 34B,* 4659–4660.

Feigon, J. (1981). A sibling group program. *Sibling Information Network Newsletter, 1,* 2.

Ferrari, M. (1984). Chronic illness: Psychosocial effects on siblings—1: Chronically ill boys. *Journal of Child Psychology and Psychiatry, 25,* 459–476.

Ferrari, M. (1987). The diabetic child and well sibling: Risks to the well child's self-concept. *Children's Health Care, 15,* 141–148.

Fewell, R.R., & Vadasy, P.F. (1986). *Families of handicapped children: Needs and supports across the lifespan.* Austin, TX: PRO-ED.

Fotheringham, J., Skelton, M., & Hodinott, B. (1971). *The retarded child and his family* (Monograph Series II). Toronto: Ontario Institute for Studies in Education.

Fowle, C. (1968). The effect of the severely mentally retarded child on the family. *American Journal of Mental Deficiency, 73,* 468–473.

Gabel, H., McDowell, J., & Cerreto, M.C. (1983). Family adaptation to the handicapped infant. In S.G. Garwood & R.R. Fewell (Ed.), *Educating handicapped infants: Issues in development and intervention* (pp. 455–493). Rockville, MD: Aspen Publishers Inc.

Gath, A. (1972). The mental health of siblings of congenitally abnormal children. *Journal of Child Psychology and Psychiatry, 13,* 211–218.

Gath, A. (1973). The school age of siblings of mongol children. *British Journal of Psychiatry, 123,* 161–167.

Gath, A. (1974). Siblings reactions to mental handicap: A comparison of brothers and sisters of mongol children. *Journal of Child Psychology and Psychiatry, 15,* 187–198.

Gath, A., & Gumley, D. (1987). Retarded children and their siblings. *Journal of Child Psychology and Psychiatry, 28,* 715–730.

Gayton, W., Friedman, S., Tavormina, J., & Tucker, F. (1977). Psychological test findings of patients, siblings, and parents. *Pediatrics, 59,* 888–894.

Gogan, J.L., & Slavin, L. (1981). Interviews with brothers and sisters. In G.P. Koocher & J.E. O'Malley (Eds.), *The Damocles syndrome: Psychosocial consequences of surviving childhood cancer* (pp. 101–111). New York: McGraw-Hill.

Graliker, B., Fischler, K., & Koch, R. (1962). Teenage reactions to mentally retarded siblings. *American Journal of Mental Deficiency, 66,* 838–843.

Grossman, F.K. (1972). *Brothers and sisters of retarded children.* Syracuse, NY: Syracuse University Press.

Gruszka, M.A. (1988). Family functioning and sibling adjustment in families with a handicapped child. Unpublished doctoral dissertation, University of Rhode Island, Kingston.

Harris, S.L. (1983). *Families of the developmentally disabled: A guide to behavioral intervention.* Elmsford, NY: Pergamon.

Hauser, S.T., Jacobson, A.M., Wertlieb, D., Brink, S., & Wentworth, S. (1985). The contribution of family and environment to perceived competence and illness adjustment in diabetic and acutely ill adolescents. *Family Relations, 34,* 99–108.

Hayden, V. (1974). The other children. *Exceptional Parent, 4,* 26–29.

James, S.D., & Egel, A.L. (1986). A direct prompting strategy for increasing reciprocal interactions between handicapped and nonhandicapped siblings. *Journal of Applied Behavior Analysis, 19,* 173–186.

Kaplan, F., & Colombatto, J. (1966). Headstart program for siblings of mentally retarded children. *Mental Retardation, 4,* 30–32.

Kazak, A. E., & Clark, M.W. (1986). Stress in families of children with myelomeningocele. *Developmental Medicine and Child Neurology, 28,* 220–228.

Klein, S.D. (1972). Brother to sister: Sister to brother. *Exceptional Parent, 2,* 10–15.

Koch, H.L. (1960). The relation of certain formal attributes of siblings to attitudes held toward each other and toward their parents. *Monographs of the Society for Research in Child Development, 25*(4), 1–124.

LaVigne, J.V., & Ryan, M. (1979). Psychologic adjustment of siblings of children with chronic illness. *Pediatrics, 63,* 616–627.

Lawson, A., & Ingleby, J.D. (1974). Daily routines of preschool children: Effects of age, birth order, sex, social class, and developmental correlates. *Psychological Medicine, 4,* 399–415.

Leanza, V.F. (1970). Tension in the adjustment of normal siblings of mildly retarded children (Doctoral dissertation, Case Western Reserve University 1970). *Dissertation Abstracts International, 31A,* 2739.

Lobato, D. (1981). Multiple assessment of a workshop program for siblings of handicapped children. Unpublished doctoral dissertation, University of Massachusetts, Amherst.

Lobato, D. (1983). Siblings of handicapped children: A review. *Journal of Autism and Developmental Disorders, 13,* 347–364.

Lobato, D. (1985). Preschool siblings of handicapped children: Impact of peer support and training. *Journal of Autism and Developmental Disorders, 9,* 287–296.

Lobato, D., Barbour, L., Hall, L.J., & Miller, C.T. (1987). Psychosocial characteristics of preschool siblings of handicapped and nonhandicapped children. *Journal of Abnormal Child Psychology, 15,* 329–338.

Lobato, D., Faust, D., & Spirito, A. (1988). Examining the effects of chronic disease and disability on children's sibling relationships. *Journal of Pediatric Psychology, 13,* 389–407.

Lobato, D., Miller, C.T., Barbour, L., & Hall, L.J. (in press). Preschool siblings of handicapped children: Interactions with mothers, brothers, and sisters. *Research in Developmental Disabilities.*

Lobato, D., & Tlaker, A. (1985). Sibling intervention with a retarded child. *Education and Treatment of Children, 8,* 221–228.

Longstreth, L.E., Longstreth, G.V., Ramirez, C., & Fernandez, G. (1975). The ubiquity of big brother. *Child Development, 46,* 769–772.

McHale, S.M., Sloan, J., & Simeonsson, R.J. (1986). Sibling relationships of children with autistic, mentally retarded, and nonhandicapped brothers and sisters. *Journal of Autism and Developmental Disorders, 16,* 399–413.

Meyer, D.J., Vadasy, P.F., & Fewell, R.R. (1985). *Living with a brother or sister with special needs: A book for sibs.* Seattle: University of Washington Press.

Miller, N., & Cantwell, D.P. (1976). Siblings as therapists: A behavioral approach. *American Journal of Psychiatry, 133,* 447–450.

Moos, R.H. (1984). *Coping with physical illness: New directions.* New York: Plenum.

Morris, L.R., & Schulz, L. (1989). *Creative play activities for children with disabilities: A resource for teachers and parents.* Champaign, IL: Human Kinetics Books.

Murphy, A., Pueschel, S.M., Duffy, T., & Brady, E. (1976). Meeting with brothers and sisters of children with Down's syndrome. *Children Today, 5,* 20–23.

Newson, J., & Newson, E. (1970). *Four years old in an urban community.* London: Penguin Press.

Newson, J., & Newson, E. (1976). *Seven years old in the home environment.* London: Penguin Press.

Perrin, E.C., & Gerrity, P.S. (1981). There's a demon in your belly: Children's understanding of illness. *Pediatrics, 67,* 841–849.

Potter, P.C., & Roberts, M.C. (1984). Children's perceptions of chronic illness: The roles of disease symptoms, cognitive development, and information. *Journal of Pediatric Psychology, 9,* 13–27.

Powell, T.H., & Ogle, P.A. (1985). *Brothers & sisters—A special part of exceptional families.* Baltimore: Paul H. Brookes Publishing Co.

Powell, T.H., Salzberg, C.L., Rule, S., Levy, S., & Itzkowitz, J.S. (1983). Teaching mentally retarded children to play with their siblings using parents as trainers. *Education and Treatment of Children, 6,* 343–362.

Robinson, N., & Robinson, H. (1976). *The mentally retarded child.* New York: McGraw-Hill.

Schreibman, L., O'Neill, R.E., & Koegel, R.L. (1983). Behavioral training for siblings of autistic children. *Journal of Applied Behavior Analysis, 16,* 129–138.

Simeonsson, R.J., & McHale, S.M. (1981). Review: Research on handicapped children: Sibling relationships. *Child: Care, Health, and Development, 7,* 153–171.

Steinhausen, H., Schindler, H., & Stephan, H. (1983). Correlates of psychopathology in sick children: An empirical model. *Journal of the American Academy of Child Psychiatry, 22,* 559–564.

Stoneman, Z., Brody, G.H., Davis, C.H., & Crapps, J.M. (1987). Mentally retarded children and their older same-sex siblings: Naturalistic in-home observations. *American Journal of Mental Retardation, 92,* 290–298.

Stoneman, Z., Brody, G.H., Davis, C.H., & Crapps, J.M. (1988). Childcare responsibilities, peer relations, and sibling conflict: Older siblings of mentally retarded children. *American Journal of Mental Retardation, 93,* 174–183.

Stoneman, Z., Brody, G.H., Davis, C.H., & Crapps, J.M. (1989). Role relations between children who are mentally retarded and their older siblings: Observations in three in-home contexts. *Research in Developmental Disabilities, 10,* 61–76.

Sullivan, R.C. (1979). Siblings of autistic children. *Journal of Autism and Developmental Disorders, 9,* 287–296.

Sutton-Smith, B. (1982). Birth-order and sibling status effects. In M.E. Lamb & B. Sutton-Smith (Eds.), *Sibling relationships: Their nature and significance across the lifespan* (pp. 153–165). Hillsdale, NJ: Lawrence Erlbaum Associates.

Sutton-Smith, B., & Rosenberg, R.B. (1970). *The sibling.* New York: Holt, Rinehart & Winston.

Svelze, M., & Keenan, V. (1981). Changes in family support networks over the life cycle of mentally retarded persons. *American Journal of Mental Deficiency, 86,* 267–274.

Tew, B., & Laurence, K.M. (1973). Mothers, brothers, and sisters of patients with spina bifida. *Developmental Medicine and Child Neurology, 15,* 69–76.

Townes, B.D., & Wold, D.A. (1977). Childhood leukemia. In E. Pattison (Ed.), *The experience of dying* (pp. 138–143). Englewood Cliffs, NJ: Prentice-Hall.

Tritt, S.G., & Esses, L.M. (1988). Psychosocial adaptation of siblings of children with chronic medical illnesses. *American Journal of Orthopsychiatry, 58,* 211–220.

U.S. Department of Health and Human Services. (1988). *Report to Congress and the Secretary by the Task Force on Technology Dependent Children* (Vols. 1–2, DHHS Publication No. 88-2171). Washington, DC: U.S. Government Printing Office.

Wagner, M.E., Schubert, H.J.P., & Schubert, D.S.P. (1979). Sibships: Constellation effects on psychosocial development, creativity, and health. In H.W. Reese & L.P. Lipsitt (Eds.), *Advances in child development and behavior* (Vol. 14, pp. 57–149). New York: Academic Press.

Wagner, M.E., Schubert, H.J.P., & Schubert, D.S.P. (1985). Effects of sibling spacing on intelligence, interfamilial relations, psychosocial characteristics, and mental and physical health. In H.W. Reese (Ed.), *Advances in child development and behavior* (Vol. 19, pp. 149–206). New York: Academic Press.

Walker, L.S., Ortiz-Valdes, J.A., & Newbrough, J.R. (1989). The role of maternal employment and depression in the psychological adjustment of chronically ill, mentally retarded, and well-children. *Journal of Pediatric Psychology, 14,* 357–370.

Weinrott, M.R. (1974). A training program in behavior modification for siblings of the retarded. *American Journal of Orthopsychiatry, 44,* 362–375.

Whitman, P., & Lobato, D. (1983, October). *Teaching instructional and play skills to preschool siblings of handicapped infants and toddlers.* Paper presented at the annual Berkshire Conference on Applied Behavior Analysis and Therapy, Amherst, MA.

Wikler, L. (1986). Periodic stresses in families of children with mental retardation. *American Journal of Mental Deficiency, 90,* 703–706.

Wikler, L., Wasow, M., & Hatfield, E. (1981). Chronic sorrow revisited: Attitudes of patients and professionals about adjustment to mental retardation. *American Journal of Orthopsychiatry, 51,* 63–70.

Wilson, J., Blacher, J., & Baker, B.L. (1989). Siblings of children with severe handicaps. *Mental Retardation, 27*(3), 167–173.

ANNOTATED BIBLIOGRAPHY

Bouchard, L. (1969) *The boy who wouldn't talk*. Garden City, NY: Doubleday.

Condition: Visual Impairment

Summary: Upon arriving in New York City from Puerto Rico, Carlos is lonely and frustrated with his inability to learn English and decides to only communicate through drawing pictures and making gestures. Then he meets Ricky, a boy with blindness who can't find his way home. Carlos finds that he must speak to his new friend in order to communicate with him. The two boys share special moments such as Carlos' first exposure to braille books and an exploration of a park for the blind. Carlos returns home and is finally able to speak with his family.

Brightman, A. (1976). *Like me*. Boston: Little, Brown.

Condition: Mental Retardation

Summary: A young boy explores the differences that exist among people. His self-awareness of his own mental retardation facilitates a deeper understanding of the emotions and thoughts that individuals with disabilities experience. The strongest aspect of this is the colorful photographs of children in a variety of social and recreational settings.

Brown, T. (1984). *Someone special, just like you*. New York: Holt, Rinehart & Winston.

Condition: General Handicaps

Summary: This book contains photographs of young children having fun in a variety of activities. Many of the children pictured do not appear to have particular, visible problems, while others do. The text and photos emphasize the similarities between children.

This annotated bibliography was compiled with the assistance of Cheryl D. Cho, Brown University.

Cairo, S. (1985). *Our brother has Down's syndrome.* Toronto: Annick Press Ltd.

Condition: Down Syndrome/Mental Retardation

Summary: Two sisters relate the joy and difficulties that come with being the sibling of a child with Down syndrome. Even though Jai has trouble climbing stairs and goes to a special play group, the three children still find pleasure in reading stories and walking along the beach with one another. This story emphasizes the strengths of a relationship with a sibling with a disability.

Christopher, M. (1975). *Glue fingers.* Boston: Little, Brown.

Condition: Speech Impairment

Summary: Even though Billy Joe is an outstanding athlete, he fears joining the football team. He is afraid that he will be ostracized because he stutters, but his older brothers finally convince him that his speech problem need not affect his enjoyment of football. Upon making a key pass and scoring, rather than jeering at his stuttering, Billy Joe finds that the crowd is cheering at his impressive play.

Clifton, L. (1980). *My friend Jacob.* New York: E.P. Dutton.

Condition: Mental Retardation

Summary: Jacob and Sam are neighbors and best friends. Though Jacob is much older than Sam, there is a lot that they teach each other. Jacob's a great basketball player , but Sam remembers things a lot better than Jacob. The day Sam remembers to knock before entering becomes a memorable day for the two of them.

Donahue, P., & Capellaro, H. (1975). *Germs make me sick: A health handbook for kids.* New York: Alfred A. Knopf.

Condition: Common Contagious Illnesses

Summary: This book contains explanations of common, acute contagious illnesses and their treatment. It is a good source of information regarding more common ailments such as pneumonia, chicken pox, German measles, and the flu.

Fanshawe, E. (1975). *Rachel.* Scarsdale, NY: Bradbury.

Condition: Orthopedic Impairment

Summary: Rachel is a typical young girl. The most remarkable aspect about her is that she must use a wheelchair to get around and do the things other children her age do. The full, happy life she leads is inspirational for those who feel limited by their handicap.

Fassler, J. (1969). *One little girl.* New York: Human Sciences.

Condition: Intellectual Impairment

Summary: Laurie is involved with many things, but often takes a long time to learn them. After taking a psychological examination, and being diagnosed as a slow learner, Laurie remains a happy, well-adjusted child thanks to plenty of emphasis on her positive attributes by those around her.

Fassler, J. (1975). *Howie helps himself.* Chicago: Whitman.

Condition: Cerebral Palsy

Summary: Assistance from others is common for Howie. His biggest wish is to learn how to work his own wheelchair independently. Howie succeeds and, with his father, celebrates this long-awaited milestone.

Glazzard, M.H. (1978). *Meet Camille and Danille, they're special persons.* Lawrence, KS: H & H Enterprises.

Condition: Hearing Impaired

Summary: Besides being twins, Camille and Danille are also hearing impaired. But, with the use of speech training, lip reading, and hearing aids, they are able to attend school with hearing children.

Glazzard, M.H. (1978). *Meet Scott, he's a special person.* Lawrence, KS: H & H Enterprises

Condition: Learning Disability

Summary: This book introduces the reader to a variety of teaching methods. Even though Scott enjoys art and plays outside with the other children, he requires some unusual teaching methods to help him learn in a different way. The special teacher introduces him to ways of learning such as drawing words in sand and reading aloud to a tape recorder.

Goodsell, J. (1965). *Katie's magic glasses.* Boston: Houghton Mifflin.

Condition: Visual Impairment

Summary: For 5-year-old Katie, everything is often just a blur. A visit to the doctor is followed up by an appointment with an ophthalmologist who informs her that she will be receiving a pair of magic glasses soon. In preparation for what is in store, Katie tries on her father's glasses that make her feel sick. Katie decides that she is no longer looking forward to receiving her own magical glasses, but abruptly changes her mind when they arrive and her surroundings take on previously unknown sharpness.

Griese, A. (1969). *At the mouth of the luckiest river.* New York: Crowell.

Condition: Orthopedic Impairment

Summary: Set in Alaska, young Tatlek, an Athabascan Indian, despite having a weak, misshapen foot, leads a happy life and believes that the good spirits that his grandfather has told him about are watching over him. He recognizes his problems and also learns to compensate for them as he develops his skills at wrestling, learns to push a sled, and confronts the village's crooked medicine man.

Hirsh, K. (1977). *My sister.* Minneapolis: Carol Rhoda Books.

Condition: Mental Retardation

Summary: The activities and social relationships of a boy and his older sister with mental retardation are compared. A variety of emotions arise as the family takes a vacation and the siblings interact with one another.

Jampolsky, G.G., & Taylor, P. (Eds.). (1978). *There is a rainbow behind every dark cloud.* Tiburon, CA: Center for Attitudinal Healing.

Condition: Cancer

Summary: This is a collection of artwork—drawings and words—of children who have had cancer.

Jampolsky, G.G., & Taylor, P. (Eds.). (1982). *Another look at the rainbow: Straight from the siblings.* Tiburon, CA: Center for Attitudinal Healing.

Condition: Cancer

Summary: Similar to their first volume, this collection focuses on the experiences of children whose brothers and sisters have had cancer.

Jupo, F. (1967). *Atu, the silent one.* New York: Holiday House.

Condition: Speech Impairment

Summary: Set in a time long ago, Atu is an African bushman who cannot speak. He is loved by the other members of his tribe and is known for his ability to communicate artistically through drawings. Atu develops not only into a great hunter, but also into the pictorial storyteller of the tribe's successes.

Keats, E. (1971). *Apt. 3.* New York: Macmillan

Condition: Visual Impairment

Summary: Kept inside all day due to rain, two brothers decide to track down the source of music that they can hear in their apartment building. Their investigating brings them to the door of a blind man playing his harmonica. Captivated by the man's ability to use hearing as a tool for learning about the world, they invite him on a walk, and the three become fast friends.

Lasker, J. (1974). *He's my brother.* Chicago: Whitman.

Condition: Learning Disability

Summary: Jamie's difficulties associated with his learning disability are explored by his older brother in this story. The book portrays Jamie's difficulties in school with academics and with peers. The support of his parents, who emphasize his abilities, is a strength of this story.

Lenski, Lois. (1952). *We live in the south.* Philadelphia: J.P. Lippincott.

Condition: Cardiac Problems

Summary: Seven-year-old Evelina has had numerous visits to doctors regarding her enlarged heart. Her frequent chest pains are met with insensitivity from her peers and poor communication between her mother and siblings regarding her problems. Damaged feelings and the unawareness of others toward Evelina's special needs result.

Nadas, B.P. (1975). *Danny's song.* New York: Hubbard Scientific.

Condition: Physical Disabilities

Summary: Danny has a physical disability and needs leg braces and crutches. His accomplishments become the focus of this book.

Naylor, P. (1967). *Jennifer Jean, the cross-eyed queen.* Minneapolis: Lerner

Condition: Visual Impairment

Summary: Due to an inward-turned eye, 4-year-old Jennifer Jean squints and tilts her head in order to see. Even though other children tease her, Jennifer Jean maintains her spirit. Jennifer begins wearing a patch, then eye glasses, and finally does regular eye exercises to improve her sight.

Newth, P. (1981). *Roly goes exploring.* New York: Putnam Publishing Company.

Condition: Visual Impairment

Summary: Written in both Braille and standard type, this book is meant for both sighted and blind children. Based on the theme of geometric shapes, it contains pictures intended to be touched as well as seen.

Ominsky, E. (1977). *Jon O.: A special boy.* Englewood Cliffs, NJ: Prentice-Hall.

Condition: Mental Retardation

Summary: The limitations and myths associated with Down syndrome are described in this story about Jon O. Participating in a full active life, Jon O. acknowledges the difficulties associated with his disability as his home life and time with friends at school and the associated pleasures are described.

Peterson, W. (1977). *I have a sister, my sister is deaf.* New York: Harper & Row.

Condition: Hearing Impaired

Summary: Narrated by an older sister, this book portrays the difficulties and joys of life with a younger sister who is hearing impaired.

Rosenberg, M.R. (1983). *My friend Leslie.* New York: Lothrop, Lee, & Shepard Books.

Condition: Multiple Sensory and Physical Impairments

Summary: Leslie and Karin attend kindergarten in the same school and have been friends for a long time. Despite Leslie's visual, hearing, and co-ordination problems, the girls enjoy similar activities at school and find comfort in their friendship.

Silverstein, A., & Silverstein, V.B. (1978). *Itch, sniffle, and sneeze: All about asthma, hay fever and other allergies.* New York: Four Winds Press.

Condition: Asthma and Allergies

Summary: In a comical light, this book discusses what allergies, hay fever, and asthma are and how to cope with them.

Smith, L.B. (1977). *A special kind of sister.* New York: Holt, Rinehart & Winston.

Condition: Mental Retardation

Summary: This story focuses on the experience of being a sibling to a child with a handicap. The feelings an older sister undergoes in response to having a brother with mental retardation and chronic illness prompts her to fake her own illness in order to gain parental attention. The reaction of the girl's peers as well as public perception to mental retardation are discussed.

Sobol, H.L. (1977). *My brother Steven is retarded.* New York: Macmillan.

Condition: Mental Retardation

Summary: In this story, the narrator, an 11-year-old girl, reveals the mixed emotions she feels toward her older brother with mental retardation. She experiences many positive and negative feelings. The girl thinks again about an old fear that retardation might be contagious.

Stein, S.B. (1974). *About Handicaps: An Open Family Book For Parents and Children Together.* New York: Walker and Co.

Condition: General Handicaps

Summary: Intended for parents and children, this book exposes the reader to a variety of handicaps and helps make the topic of disabilities more comfortable for discussion. Witnessing the handicaps of others brings out Matthew's own fears regarding his physical imperfections. He fears that if other people discover that his toes curl up, people will also stare at him. Then he realizes that all kinds of disabilities make people special, and that this should not be feared.

Turnbull, A.S. (1968). *The white lark.* Boston: Houghton Mifflin.

Condition: Physical Disability

Summary: Following an accident, Suzy has had to depend upon leg braces to get around. While visiting her aunt in America, she meets a man who was born with short legs. Together, Suzy and her new friend share stories of their experiences of being handicapped.

Vance, M. (1956). *Windows for Rosemary.* New York: E.P. Dutton

Condition: Visual Impairment

Summary: This book explores the adjustments that are necessary for dealing with blindness. Rosemary depends upon the location of furniture to make her way around the house and finds that even her friends have misconceptions about her blindness. Her warm, up-beat family are strengths.

White, P. (1978). *Janet at school.* New York: Harper & Row.

Condition: Physical Disability

Summary: This book reveals the difficulties and pleasures of a young girl with spina bifida. The story follows her through time at home, school, and on a camping trip.

Wolf, B. (1974). *Don't feel sorry for Paul.* New York: J.B. Lippincott.

Condition: Physical Disability

Summary: Accompanied by photographs, this book dispels the myths associated with prosthetic devices as it follows Paul, a second-grader who has physical handicaps, and his family through a variety of day-to-day activities.

Wolf, B. (1977). *Anna's silent world.* Philadelphia: J.B. Lippincott.

Condition: Hearing Impaired

Summary: Six-year-old Anna attends first grade and ballet class despite her severe hearing impairment. This book explores the process and tools involved with learning to communicate through speech and lip reading.

INDEX